Inventors Who Changed the World

J. Robert Oppenheimer
The Brain Behind the Bomb

Glenn Scherer and Marty Fletcher

MyReportLinks.com Books
an imprint of

Enslow Publishers, Inc.
Box 398, 40 Industrial Road
Berkeley Heights, NJ 07922
USA

MyReportLinks.com Books, an imprint of Enslow Publishers, Inc. MyReportLinks® is a registered trademark of Enslow Publishers, Inc.

Library of Congress Cataloging-in-Publication Data
Scherer, Glenn.
   J. Robert Oppenheimer: the brain behind the bomb / Glenn Scherer and Marty Fletcher.
       p. cm. — (Inventors who changed the world)
   Includes bibliographical references and index.
   ISBN-13: 978-1-59845-050-7
   ISBN-10: 1-59845-050-6
   1. Oppenheimer, J. Robert, 1904–1967—Juvenile literature. 2. Atomic bomb—United States—History—Juvenile literature. 3. Physicists—United States—Biography—Juvenile literature. I. Fletcher, Marty. II. Title.
   QC16.O62S36 2007
   530.092—dc22
   [B]
                                        2006020820
Printed in the United States of America

10 9 8 7 6 5 4 3 2 1

To Our Readers:
Through the purchase of this book, you and your library gain access to the Report Links that specifically back up this book.

The Publisher will provide access to the Report Links that back up this book and will keep these Report Links up to date on **www.myreportlinks.com** for five years from the book's first publication date.

We have done our best to make sure all Internet addresses in this book were active and appropriate when we went to press. However, the author and the Publisher have no control over, and assume no liability for, the material available on those Internet sites or on other Web sites they may link to.

The usage of the MyReportLinks.com Books Web site is subject to the terms and conditions stated on the Usage Policy Statement on **www.myreportlinks.com**.

A password may be required to access the Report Links that back up this book. The password is found on the bottom of page 4 of this book.

Any comments or suggestions can be sent by e-mail to comments@myreportlinks.com or to the address on the back cover.

CONTENTS

MyReportLinks.com Books
Great Books, Great Links, Great for Research!

The Internet sites featured in this book can save you hours of research time. These Internet sites—we call them **"Report Links"**—are constantly changing, but we keep them up to date on our Web site.

When you see this "Approved Web Site" logo, you will know that we are directing you to a great Internet site that will help you with your research.

Give it a try! Type http://www.myreportlinks.com into your browser, click on the series title and enter the password, then click on the book title, and scroll down to the Report Links listed for this book.

The Report Links will bring you to great source documents, photographs, and illustrations. MyReportLinks.com Books save you time, feature Report Links that are kept up to date, and make report writing easier than ever! A complete listing of the Report Links can be found on pages 118–119 at the back of the book.

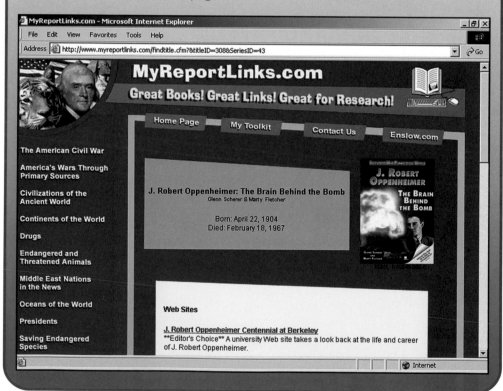

Please see "To Our Readers" on the copyright page for important information about this book, the MyReportLinks.com Web site, and the Report Links that back up this book.

Please enter JRN1849 if asked for a password.

Science is not everything,
but science is very beautiful.

—J. Robert Oppenheimer

IMPORTANT DATES

1904—*April 22:* J. Robert Oppenheimer is born in New York City to Julius and Ella Oppenheimer.

1915—Becomes a member of the New York Mineralogical Society; gives a geology lecture a year later at the age of twelve.

1911
–1921—Attends Ethical Culture School, New York City.

1922
–1925—Earns his Harvard University undergraduate degree in just three years, graduating summa cum laude.

1925
–1927—Studies abroad at Cavendish Laboratory, Cambridge University, England, and George-August-Universität, Göttingen, Germany, earning his doctorate in physics.

1929—Takes up teaching position at the California Institute of Technology and the University of California at Berkeley; develops a world-class theoretical physics department at Berkeley over the next decade.

1936
–1942—Oppenheimer is involved with the American Communist party, though it is doubtful that he was a member.

1939—Oppenheimer publishes one of the great papers in twentieth-century physics, theorizing the existence of black holes.

1939—*September 1:* World War II begins. The Nazis under Adolf Hitler work to develop an atomic bomb.

—*October 11:* A letter from physicists Albert Einstein and Leo Szilard (pronounced SIL ard) warns United States president Franklin Roosevelt that the Nazis are building an atomic bomb. Roosevelt launches an atomic bomb project to beat the Nazis.

1940—Oppenheimer marries Katherine Puening.

1941—*December 7:* Japanese attack Pearl Harbor. The United States declares war on Japan, then on Germany.

1942—*October 15:* Oppenheimer is appointed to establish and run the top secret Los Alamos Laboratory, in New Mexico. Over the next three years, he leads a team of scientists in developing the first atomic bomb.

1945—*May 7:* Germany surrenders to the Allies, so it will no longer be a target for the atomic bomb developed by the United States.

—*July 16:* The Trinity test in Alamogordo, New Mexico, is the first successful test of the plutonium atom bomb.

—*August 6:* A U-235 atomic bomb is dropped on the Japanese city of Hiroshima, and an estimated 70,000 people die from the initial blast.

—*August 9:* A plutonium atomic bomb is dropped on the Japanese city of Nagasaki, and an estimated 40,000 people die from the initial blast.

—*August 14:* World War II ends with Japan's agreement to surrender unconditionally, although the formal surrender takes place on September 2.

—*November 2:* Oppenheimer gives a farewell speech to fellow physicists at Los Alamos, denouncing the use of atomic weapons in future warfare.

1945 –1952 —Oppenheimer is one of the most important and respected advisors on national and international atomic policy.

1946 —Receives a Presidential Citation and a Medal of Merit for his direction of the Los Alamos Laboratory.

1947 –1966 —Heads the Institute for Advanced Study in Princeton, New Jersey.

1953 —Oppenheimer is accused of having been a Communist party member, possibly being a spy, and leaking atomic bomb secrets to the Soviets.

1954 —*June 29:* The Atomic Energy Commission formally strips Oppenheimer of his top secret security clearance, ending his involvement with the atomic energy program.

1963 —President Lyndon Johnson presents Oppenheimer with the prestigious Fermi Award, recognizing his loyalty to his nation. (President John F. Kennedy had chosen Oppenheimer for the award; President Johnson succeeded Kennedy following Kennedy's assassination.)

1967 —*February 18:* J. Robert Oppenheimer dies from throat cancer, at the age of sixty-two, in Princeton, New Jersey.

1994 —The Federal Bureau of Investigation (F.B.I.) publicly announces that its allegations that Oppenheimer had shared secrets with the Soviets were unfounded.

2004 —*April 28:* The United States Senate passes a resolution recognizing "the loyal service and outstanding contributions of J. Robert Oppenheimer to the United States and calling on the Secretary of Energy to observe the 100th anniversary of Dr. Oppenheimer's birth with appropriate programs at the Department of Energy and Los Alamos National Laboratory."

FIRE IN THE DESERT

A tense voice rang out in the desert stillness: "Zero minus ten seconds." The countdown continued: zero minus nine seconds, eight seconds, seven seconds, six seconds, five, four, three, two, one, zero. . . .

Then a burst of atomic fire lit up the New Mexico sky. It was 5:30 A.M. on July 16, 1945, and the first atomic bomb had just been detonated, starting the nuclear age and changing the world forever.

New York Times reporter William L. Laurence, who was the only journalist at the scene, described the horrific explosion this way:

CHAPTER

1

[It was] a sunrise such as the world had never seen, a great green supersun climbing in a fraction of a second to a height of more than eight thousand feet, rising ever higher until it touched the clouds, lighting up earth and sky all around with a dazzling luminosity. Up it went, a great ball of fire about a mile in diameter, changing colors as it kept shooting upward, from deep purple to orange, expanding, growing bigger, rising as it expanded, an elemental force freed from its bonds after being chained for billions of years. For a fleeting instant the color was unearthly green . . . It was as though the earth had opened and the skies had split. One felt as though one were present at the moment of creation when God said: "Let there be light."[1]

This moment marked the dawn of a new and powerful weapon. At the Trinity atomic bomb test in the New Mexico desert that morning, the most destructive power yet created by human beings was unleashed. The man most responsible for this bomb was a theoretical physicist who stood with his fellow scientists about six miles away from where the bomb exploded. His name was J. Robert Oppenheimer, and he leaned his weight against a post in a bunker made of earth, concrete, and wood, and watched silently. His face was first hit by a tremendous blast of light. Thirty seconds later,

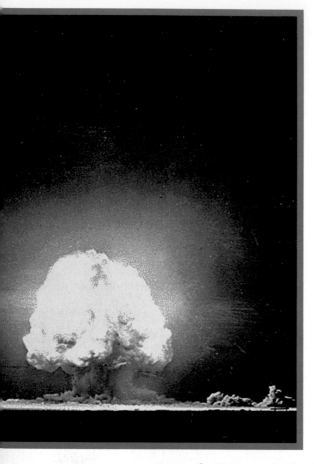

◀ On July 16, 1945, the desert near Alamogordo, New Mexico, was the site of the first atomic bomb detonation. The Trinity test unleashed a destructive power never before seen by human-kind. Dr. J. Robert Oppenheimer was the man responsible for overseeing the construction of the world's first atomic weapon.

he and others in the bunker were struck by a wind of hurricane force, then by a deafening roar, louder and longer than any thunder ever heard on earth.

Oppenheimer watched as a great mushroom cloud rose higher and higher. It climbed up to 41,000 feet above the ground, higher than Mount Everest, before finally fading away into the dawn's gloom. Oppenheimer's response is reported to have been "It worked," spoken to his brother Frank, also a physicist.[2] Later, Oppenheimer would tell journalists that at that moment he was reminded of a passage from the *Bhagavad Gita,* an ancient Hindu book of scripture: "I am become Death, the shatterer of worlds."[3]

Dr. J. Robert Oppenheimer and General Leslie Groves are photographed at the Trinity test site. General Groves was the senior official in charge of the Manhattan Engineer Project, the code name for the construction of the atomic bomb.

Out in the desert at ground zero, the center of the explosion, the heat from the bomb was calculated to be 100,000,000°F, three times the temperature at the center of the sun. All plant and animal life for a mile around had been killed, burned up, or completely obliterated. An antelope herd that had been seen by observers from a plane only moments before the bomb detonated had vanished—and so had every cactus, rattlesnake, jackrabbit, and blade of grass in the area.

The entire atomic bomb site around ground zero was also filled with invisible but deadly radiation, a product of this new kind of bomb. Any living thing near ground zero that did not die in the blast or from the intense heat would most likely die from radiation sickness in a matter of days or weeks.

Within a month, the atomic bomb would be used again, though this time it would kill more than rabbits and antelope. It would be used against the Japanese, with whom the United States was at war. The two bombs dropped on the Japanese cities of Hiroshima and Nagasaki would eventually claim the lives of 340,000 human beings and end World War II.

⊖The Top Secret Manhattan Project

For more than two years, J. Robert Oppenheimer had led the top secret Manhattan Project in a race against Nazi Germany to build the first nuclear weapon. The Manhattan Project was the biggest construction project to that time ever taken on by civilization.

The race against Adolf Hitler and the Nazis had begun in 1939. In June of that year, concerned scientists, including the renowned physicist Albert Einstein, wrote a letter to Franklin Delano Roosevelt, the president of the United States, warning him that the Nazis were planning to build a new type of superbomb. This bomb would be hundreds of times more powerful than any ever built.

A New Kind of Bomb

This new atomic bomb would be powered by something called nuclear fission. A neutron, a kind of subatomic particle, would be forced to collide with the nucleus of an unstable plutonium or uranium atom. An unstable atom is one that does not have enough binding energy to hold the nucleus together permanently. Unstable atoms emit radiation and are known as radioactive atoms. When the neutron hit the atom, its nucleus would split, giving off massive amounts of energy and more neutrons. Those neutrons would then collide with other nuclei of other unstable plutonium or uranium atoms, causing them to divide in what is called a chain reaction. So much energy would be released by this chain reaction that a bomb powerful enough to destroy an entire city could be made from just a few pounds of "fissionable" material.

President Roosevelt considered the letter from the two scientists very seriously. He then decided to put the American military and America's scientists to work to build an atomic bomb ahead of the Nazis. The resulting Manhattan Project, officially launched in 1942, employed more than 130,000 people and cost a total of nearly $2 billion. The making of this new bomb required manufacturing and research sites all over the United States, including a gigantic top secret plutonium production city and factory in Hanford, Washington, and a top secret uranium 235 (U-235) production facility and city in Oak Ridge, Tennessee. Plutonium and U-235

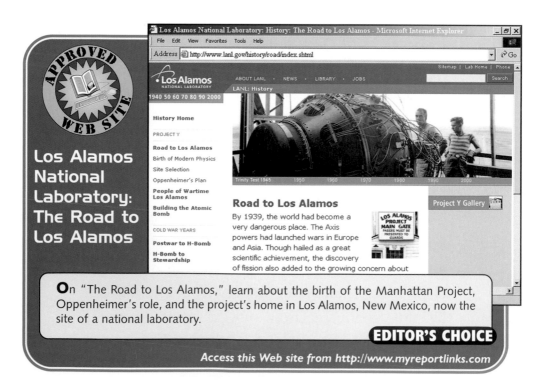

Los Alamos National Laboratory: The Road to Los Alamos

On "The Road to Los Alamos," learn about the birth of the Manhattan Project, Oppenheimer's role, and the project's home in Los Alamos, New Mexico, now the site of a national laboratory.

EDITOR'S CHOICE

Access this Web site from http://www.myreportlinks.com

were the basic fissionable atomic materials used in the bombs.

J. Robert Oppenheimer led the bomb research from a third secret place—Los Alamos, New Mexico. At the height of the Manhattan Project, thousands of scientists and their families lived and worked in Los Alamos. This place was so secret that almost no one in the United States knew about it except for the president and a few top officials.

⇒ DAWN OF THE ATOMIC AGE

With the invention of the first atomic weapon and the beginning of the atomic age, the human race entered a new period in history. It had gained the power to destroy civilization in minutes with the push of a button.

Before the successful Trinity test of the first atomic bomb in the New Mexico desert, it took the most advanced modern weaponry—thousands of soldiers and artillery pieces, or hundreds of planes and thousands of conventional bombs—to destroy even part of a great city. But a single airplane dropping just one atomic bomb could level an entire city, killing most of its population in an instant. The first bomb exploded with the force of roughly 18 kilotons, or 18,000 tons of dynamite.

Such power changed the way that nations, leaders, and people saw the world. In the decades after 1945, Oppenheimer's invention resulted in an

A Photo-Essay on the Bombing of Hiroshima and Nagasaki - Microsoft Internet Explorer

File   Edit   View   Favorites   Tools   Help

Address http://www.english.uiuc.edu/maps/poets/g_l/levine/bombing.htm

Photo by US Army
The huge atomic cloud 6 August, 1945. A Uranium bomb, the first
nuclear weapon in the world, was dropped in Hiroshima City. It
was estimated that its energy was equivalent to 15 kilotons of
TNT. Aerial photograph from the 80 kilometers away of the

A university Web site offers **A Photo-Essay on the Bombing of Hiroshima and Nagasaki,** graphic images of the atomic bombs dropped on those Japanese cities during World War II and the aftermath.

escalating arms race between the United States and the Soviet Union. These superpowers competed to build ever bigger, more sophisticated, more deadly atomic weapons.

⊜FEAR IN THE FIFTIES AND SIXTIES

The bomb's existence resulted in the construction of backyard fallout shelters by families all across the United States. These shelters were supposed to protect people in the event of an atomic bomb attack.

The bomb also forced schools across the United States to conduct regular air-raid drills in which children would hide under their desks or sit in dark hallways with their jackets pulled up over their heads. These actions would have done little to save the children or their families from a nuclear blast, but no one knew what else could be done.

The invention of the atomic bomb nearly resulted in the destruction of civilization. In 1962, the United States discovered nuclear missile installations set up by the Soviet Union in Cuba, which was just ninety miles from Florida. The Cuban Missile Crisis was a moment in the Cold War between the world's two superpowers that nearly launched World War III—a nuclear confrontation that could have devastated the entire planet.

⇒ A BUILDUP OF NUCLEAR WEAPONS

Since 1945, the world has seen nuclear proliferation, or buildup, as other nations learned how to build an atomic bomb. Today, the United States, Great Britain, France, Russia and other nations within the former Soviet Union, China, Israel, India, and Pakistan have developed their own nuclear weapons. North Korea has already tested a nuclear weapon, and there is fear that Iran will soon develop one, along with the rockets needed to deliver it. Worst of all is the threat of terrorists developing an atomic bomb that could be used anywhere in the world.

→A Man at War and a Man of Peace

J. Robert Oppenheimer was the enigmatic man who did more than anyone to bring the atomic bomb, the world's most powerful weapon of mass destruction, into existence. And yet, "Oppie," as he was known to his good friends, was not a soldier. Nor did he love war. He was a patriot who took on the monumental task of developing the atomic

▲ Dr. Oppenheimer stands near the entryway of the building housing the Institute for Advanced Study on the campus of Princeton University. It was there that the father of the atomic bomb spent his last years.

bomb in order to protect his country from the nuclear threat of the Nazis.

After the Nazi and Japanese threats to the United States disappeared at the end of World War II, Oppenheimer regarded the atomic bomb not as the ultimate weapon of war but a means of ending war for all time. He saw that the bomb was relatively easy and inexpensive to build and feared that many nations would soon construct their own bombs. Oppenheimer wanted the United Nations (UN) to control all nuclear technology and prevent all nations from having atomic weapons. He especially did not want the United States to build a super-atomic bomb, a hydrogen bomb.

Unfortunately, Oppenheimer's beliefs were not popular during the Cold War, a time when the United States and Soviet Union were jockeying for position to become the greatest world power. Some people heard Oppenheimer's talk of peace in a nuclear age as treason. They went so far as to accuse Oppenheimer of being a spy and a traitor. The United States government stripped J. Robert Oppenheimer of his security clearance, banning him from working on any top secret nuclear research. In the end, the man behind the atomic bomb found himself unable to work toward its future development as a deterrent to war.

EARLY YEARS

Julius Robert Oppenheimer was born on April 22, 1904, less than a year after the invention of the first airplane, by the Wright brothers. It was a time when many Americans lived without automobiles, relied on horses for transportation, and lacked electricity in their homes.

Robert's parents were Julius and Ella Oppenheimer, wealthy Jewish Americans who lived in New York City. Julius Oppenheimer left Germany and came to the United States in 1888 and made his living in the clothing industry, becoming a prosperous business-man. Ella Oppenheimer was a painter whose family had emigrated from Germany in the mid-1800s.

Robert Oppenheimer grew up in a spacious apartment on Manhattan's Upper West Side, overlooking the Hudson River. The apartment took up the entire floor of the building and was decorated richly with fine European furniture. The family collected

CHAPTER

2

great art, including the works of Rembrandt, Pierre-Auguste Renoir, Pablo Picasso, and Vincent van Gogh.

→ A CHILD OF PROMISE

Robert Oppenheimer's parents were well-educated intellectuals, and they recognized their son's genius right away and encouraged his scientific career. "They adored [Robert], worried about him and protected him," remembered Robert's cousin Babette Oppenheimer. "He was given every opportunity to develop along the lines of his own inclinations and at his own rate of speed."[1]

His talents were nurtured from an early age. Robert's father saw his son playing with blocks one day and immediately went out and bought him a book on architecture. At the age of five, Robert went on a trip to Germany where his grandfather gave the boy a rock collection with all the samples labeled in German. "From then on," Oppenheimer later said, "I became, in a completely childish way, an ardent mineral collector and I had, by the time I was through, quite a fine [mineral] collection."[2] Father and son especially enjoyed long hours spent rock collecting outside New York City, beneath New Jersey's Palisades cliffs.

A Childhood Steeped in Science

The family's apartment soon not only displayed paintings by famous artists, but also Robert's large and growing rock collection, with all specimens labeled with their scientific names. Julius provided his son with many books about geology. "When I was ten or twelve," Oppenheimer later recalled, "minerals, writing poems and reading, and building with blocks still—architecture—were the three themes that I did."[3]

Another gift from Robert's father opened up tremendous new horizons for the boy. It was a professional-quality microscope that became his favorite plaything. The young Robert became so adept as a chemist that his chemistry tutor asked him to spend an entire summer helping him set up a small laboratory.

Julius Oppenheimer also gave his son a type-writer, which he used to bang out letters to famous local geologists. When Robert was eleven, one of those letters so impressed a geologist that

A childhood photo of Robert Oppenheimer, left, and his younger brother, Frank. The bond between the brothers remained strong throughout their lives.

he nominated the youngster for membership in the New York Mineralogical Club. A year later, another letter arrived, inviting Robert to give a lecture to the club, made up of adults. The young Oppenheimer was afraid of facing all these adults, but his father encouraged him. So the boy went ahead and wrote a lecture on geology. When he went to the meeting and started to deliver his talk, however, the adult amateur rock collectors and professional geologists began to laugh at him. Undaunted, Robert, standing on top of a wooden box behind the podium so that he could be seen by

bio - Microsoft Internet Explorer

File   Edit   View   Favorites   Tools   Help

Address http://www.exploratorium.edu/frank/photos/photos.html

Left: Frank and brother J. Robert Oppenheimer. Center; Young Frank. Right: The budding physicist. Photos courtesy Michael Oppenheimer.

Frank Oppenheimer: Founder of the Exploratorium offers these photographs of J. Robert Oppenheimer's younger brother, who was also a noted physicist and worked on the development of the atomic bomb at Berkeley and Los Alamos. Learn more about his life and his career at the science museum he founded in San Francisco.

the audience, delivered his lecture. The audience was impressed and gave him a great round of applause.

In 1912, when Robert Oppenheimer was eight years old, his mother gave birth to a second son, Frank. Frank, too, was a gifted and pampered child. When he showed interest in the writings of Geoffrey Chaucer, an English writer of the Middle Ages, his father bought him a complete edition of the author's works, and when Frank expressed interest in playing the flute, his father hired one of the nation's finest flutists to give him private lessons. Robert and Frank were not only brothers but also best friends. Both would grow up to be theoretical physicists—and work on the Manhattan Project side by side.

A Loner at School and a Daredevil

Robert was a serious, solitary, and scholarly boy who did well in his studies at the private school he attended. He loved the world of books and of science but was picked on by the other boys in school. "He was a dreamer," said Babette Oppenheimer, "and not interested in the rough-and-tumble life of his age group. . . . he was often teased and ridiculed for not being like other fellows."[4]

Robert was uninterested in school sports. He was driven around by chauffeurs and waited on by servants. The head of the school once became so annoyed about Robert's lack of physical activity

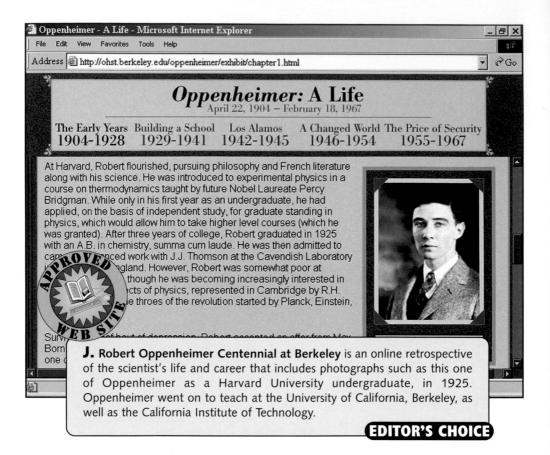

Oppenheimer - A Life - Microsoft Internet Explorer

File   Edit   View   Favorites   Tools   Help

Address   http://ohst.berkeley.edu/oppenheimer/exhibit/chapter1.html   Go

Oppenheimer: A Life
April 22, 1904 – February 18, 1967

The Early Years	Building a School	Los Alamos	A Changed World	The Price of Security
1904-1928	1929-1941	1942-1945	1946-1954	1955-1967

At Harvard, Robert flourished, pursuing philosophy and French literature along with his science. He was introduced to experimental physics in a course on thermodynamics taught by future Nobel Laureate Percy Bridgman. While only in his first year as an undergraduate, he had applied, on the basis of independent study, for graduate standing in physics, which would allow him to take higher level courses (which he was granted). After three years of college, Robert graduated in 1925 with an A.B. in chemistry, summa cum laude. He was then admitted to car[...]anced work with J.J. Thomson at the Cavendish Laboratory i[...]gland. However, Robert was somewhat poor at [...]though he was becoming increasingly interested in [...]cts of physics, represented in Cambridge by R.H. [...]e throes of the revolution started by Planck, Einstein,

Surv[...]
Born[...]
one [...]

J. Robert Oppenheimer Centennial at Berkeley is an online retrospective of the scientist's life and career that includes photographs such as this one of Oppenheimer as a Harvard University undergraduate, in 1925. Oppenheimer went on to teach at the University of California, Berkeley, as well as the California Institute of Technology.

EDITOR'S CHOICE

and his constant use of the school's elevator that he sent a note home to Robert's parents, saying, "Please teach your son to walk upstairs; he is holding up class."[5] After that, Robert tried to get more involved in sports, but he was uncoordinated and clumsy. He tried to play tennis, but did not do well and immediately quit. It seems that Robert Oppenheimer never stuck with any activity for long that he could not immediately do well in.

There was one activity he learned to love, though, and that was sailing. As teenagers, he and

Frank took daylong sailing trips on Long Island Sound, where their daredevil antics sometimes got them into trouble. Once their boat, the *Trimethy*, was nearly swept out to sea, and the boys spent five hours trying to get it back into the bay without capsizing. Robert Oppenheimer's recklessness was a characteristic that would show up again and again in his life.

➔ College Undergraduate Years

J. Robert Oppenheimer was accepted to Harvard University but, because of illness, could not attend right away. He had vacationed in Europe the summer before college, hiking and looking for minerals in the mountains of Germany. While he was there, he contracted dysentery and colitis, two diseases that kept him from beginning his freshman college year.

Sick and stuck at home, Oppenheimer turned rebellious, locking himself in his room and refusing to listen to anyone. His father asked one of the teachers at school to take his son out West to recuperate, and it turned out to be one of the happiest times of Robert Oppenheimer's life. The two rode horseback for weeks through the mountains of Colorado and New Mexico. Camping, hiking, and riding did wonders for his health, and what quickly became his love of the West would prompt him to locate the Manhattan Project's secret city of Los Alamos in the New Mexico mountains. His time out West had one unfortunate consequence, however:

It was then that Robert Oppenheimer became a chain-smoker of cigarettes, which very likely contributed to the throat cancer that killed him in 1967.

⇒ AT HARVARD

Finally, in the fall of 1922, Robert left home for Harvard University. He decided to major in chemistry, though he had considered becoming an architect, a professor of literature, a poet, and a painter. One of his friends recalls what Oppenheimer went through in college: "He found social adjustment very difficult, and I think he was often very unhappy. I suppose he was lonely and felt he didn't fit in well with the human environment."[6] Oppenheimer was able to make some friends, but he never developed a real warmth or intimacy with his classmates at Harvard. One reason for that may be because he studied so hard. He finished a four-year undergraduate chemistry program in just three years.

It was near the end of his years at Harvard that J. Robert Oppenheimer met Percy Bridgman, a famous experimental physicist. Bridgman introduced Oppenheimer to the world of theoretical and experimental physics, and suddenly Robert Oppenheimer found what he wanted to do. Physics is the science of matter and energy and their interactions. "It was the study of order, of regularity, of what makes matter harmonious and

CLIMBING MT. WILSON helped Oppenheimer, 17, recover from an illness. On trip west he fell in love with New Mexico, now owns ranch near Los Alamos.

A photograph of Robert Oppenheimer as a teenager climbing Mount Wilson is one of the images found on the **Atomic Heritage Foundation:** *Life* **Magazine, October 10, 1949** site. It includes the full text of the magazine's cover story on the famous scientist.

what makes it work,"[7] Oppenheimer later said, describing the reasons for his fascination with this branch of science.

⇒ In England

After graduating from Harvard in 1925, Oppenheimer sailed for Europe. There he began his studies in physics at the Cavendish Laboratory at Cambridge University. It says something about his extreme confidence in himself that though he was trained in chemistry, not physics, he was now challenging himself by studying at one of the most

▲ *Trinity College, Cambridge University. Robert Oppenheimer began his study of physics at Cambridge's Cavendish Laboratory, where some of the greatest minds of modern science have flourished.*

internationally acclaimed centers for experimental physics in the world.

Oppenheimer had some shortcomings in the area of mathematics, which is critically important to physics. Sometimes he would stand in front of a Cavendish Laboratory blackboard, chalk in hand for hours, unable to find answers to the equations scrawled there. His initial failures at learning theoretical physics drove him to despair and depression.

In Germany

A brief vacation on the island of Corsica, in the Mediterranean Sea, where he hiked and camped out under the stars, improved his mood greatly and propelled him toward a decision. In 1926, Oppenheimer left Cambridge and went to study at the University of Göttingen in Germany. It was a momentous decision. Oppenheimer had gotten a taste of theoretical physics at Cambridge, but at Göttingen, he was at the center of it.

The decision to go to Göttingen was a good one for another reason. During the 1920s, this university was at the heart of research into the structure of matter and atomic theory. As a child, Robert Oppenheimer had loved playing with building blocks. At Göttingen, he found that he enjoyed playing with atoms and subatomic particles, the building blocks of the universe.

Oppenheimer became especially interested in a branch of theoretical physics called quantum mechanics. Quantum mechanics is the study of how the universe works at very small scales. It looks at how subatomic particles such as electrons, protons, and neutrons behave within an atom.

➯ A NEW THEORY

Quantum mechanics replaced the overly simplistic theory of renowned physicist Niels Bohr. Bohr's theory held that an atom looked like a tiny solar system, with the nucleus acting like the sun at the center and electrons spinning around it like planets in their orbits. Instead, quantum theory said that it was impossible to know where the electrons were, only that they existed as "waves" or a "cloud" curled all around the nucleus. In the strange topsy-turvy world of quantum mechanics, it is impossible to locate an electron exactly in its path, and in fact, the electron is said to exist at every point along its path at the same time.

Oppenheimer was especially fascinated by quantum mechanics because its mathematical equations explained observable phenomena in a "harmonious, consistent and intelligible way."[8] In the twentieth century, quantum mechanics led to the development of the modern personal computer, genetic engineering, and laser technology. Inventions such as DVD and CD players and bar-code readers in supermarkets rely on quantum theory in order to work. Oppenheimer's knowledge of the mathematical laws of quantum mechanics would be absolutely essential to his future work developing the atomic bomb.

While at Göttingen, Oppenheimer wrote his first scientific paper and demonstrated that by using quantum theory, it was possible to measure the energy emitted by a radiant source, like a star or a burning candle. He also demonstrated that quantum theory could be used to identify all the

▲ *New Mexico became an important place in the life of J. Robert Oppenheimer. He went there originally to regain his health, but he came to love the land so much that he bought a ranch there. A young Oppenheimer and his horse, Crisis, are pictured at his ranch.*

elements that were being heated up. In another of his Göttingen papers, Oppenheimer explained the quantum behavior of molecules.

His work was so advanced for its time that it was understood only by the top physicists. One fellow student rated Oppenheimer as one of the three brightest students studying physics in Europe at the time, saying, "There are three young geniuses in theory here, each less intelligible to me than the others."[9]

In the spring of 1927, J. Robert Oppenheimer was awarded his doctorate with honors from Göttingen. In only two years he had gone from being a little-known college student to being one of the most respected scientists in the world in the field of theoretical physics.

PROFESSOR OPPENHEIMER

Upon returning to the United States, Oppenheimer took up teaching and research positions at two universities. He was to teach part of the year at the California Institute of Technology, known as Caltech, in Pasadena, and the rest of the year at the University of California at Berkeley, near San Francisco.

On the drive cross-country to Caltech, Oppenheimer was accompanied by his brother, Frank. The two were great friends and great physicists but known to be terrible drivers. In Colorado, with Frank driving, their convertible flipped over, and Robert broke his arm. Still disheveled from the

Oppenheimer cuts a stylish figure on the campus of the California Institute of Technology, better known as Caltech, where he taught physics.

trip and wearing a bright red arm sling, he arrived at the Caltech campus and declared, "I am Oppenheimer."[10] His grand entrance made little impression, however. A fellow professor seeing the twenty-four-year-old Oppenheimer for the first time, dressed in dusty and wrinkled old clothing, thought he "looked more like a tramp than a college professor."[11] What Oppenheimer may have lacked in appearance he made up for with his sharp mathematical genius.

Oppenheimer's arrival at Berkeley was delayed when he was diagnosed with a mild case

The Berkeley Science Review: View Image - Microsoft Internet Explorer

File   Edit   View   Favorites   Tools   Help

Address http://sciencereview.berkeley.edu/imageview.php?issue=1&article=scientistx&image=1_young_lawrence

"Regarding Scientist X," an article from the *Berkeley Science Review,* provides this photograph of Ernest Lawrence, who in 1936 became the director of the University of California at Berkeley's Radiation Laboratory and, like Oppenheimer, was involved in the development of the atomic bomb.

of tuberculosis. Again, he sought to regain his health by a stay at a ranch in New Mexico. It was a ranch that he eventually bought.

A DESERT BLOOMS

When Oppenheimer finally arrived at Berkeley, he referred to it as a theoretical physics desert because its course work in the subject was so weak. But it was a desert that bloomed under his guidance: Within a few short years—and after much hard work—Berkeley became the center for the study of theoretical physics in the United States. A year before Oppenheimer arrived at Berkeley, a young physicist from South Dakota had been appointed an assistant professor there. Ernest Lawrence went on to become the director of the Berkeley Radiation Laboratory, or Rad Lab, as it became known to those who worked there. While at Berkeley, Lawrence invented the cyclotron, a machine that used electric and magnetic fields to make particles move with enough energy to bombard the nuclei of atoms. Oppenheimer, the theoretical physicist, and Lawrence, the experimental physicist, were from vastly different backgrounds but became friends as well as colleagues.

Oppenheimer started right away trying to teach the very new and complex principles of quantum mechanics. The subject was difficult enough to begin with; it was not made any easier by Professor Oppenheimer, who often mumbled and stammered

▲ *A rare color photograph of Robert Oppenheimer during his tenure at Caltech.*

during his lectures while puffing away on a cigarette. In time, though, Oppenheimer learned to be a brilliant lecturer and teacher, and he developed a small group of students who worshipped him. Many of these highly gifted students would later join him in building the atomic bomb.

⊝ BLAZING A TRAIL IN QUANTUM MECHANICS

While teaching at Berkeley and Caltech, Oppenheimer wrote several trailblazing scientific papers in the field of quantum mechanics. The first suggested that the negatively charged electron must have its opposite counterpart in a then completely unknown, positively charged subatomic particle. Oppenheimer called this theoretical antielectron the "positron." Two years later, in 1932, experimental physicist Carl Anderson proved that the positron existed.

Oppenheimer also had an intense interest in astrophysics, the branch of astronomy dealing with the behavior, properties, and processes of celestial bodies such as planets, stars, and so on. In the 1930s, he wrote several imaginative papers theorizing about the nature of neutron stars. A neutron star is the collapsed core of a massive star that results after the star explodes at the end of its life. This explosion is known as a supernova. A neutron star is so dense and so tightly packed that all of its atoms have collapsed with only atomic nuclei remaining. Astronomers would not actually observe a real neutron star, confirming Oppenheimer's theories, until 1967.

In 1939, Oppenheimer published what has been called "one of the great papers in twentieth-century physics."[12] He and a colleague theorized the existence of black holes. A black hole occurs in outer space when a super-massive star collapses on itself. Its matter becomes so dense and its gravity so intense that nothing can ever escape from it, not even light. In 1972, astronomers confirmed Oppenheimer's theories by observing black holes for the first time.

⇒ POLITICS AND MARRIAGE

During the 1930s, Robert Oppenheimer also got involved in politics. When he learned about German physicists who were desperate to escape Nazi Germany, he contributed money to bring them to the United States. During the Great Depression, when many people were out of work, Oppenheimer came to the defense of labor unions. He supported farmworkers who were on strike for better pay, and he also supported the strikes of longshoremen working at the San Francisco docks whose wages were being cut or who were suffering layoffs. His girlfriend at the time, Jean Tatlock, influenced him to become involved in more radical politics, especially the American Communist party.

"I saw what the Depression was doing to my students," said Oppenheimer. "Often they could get

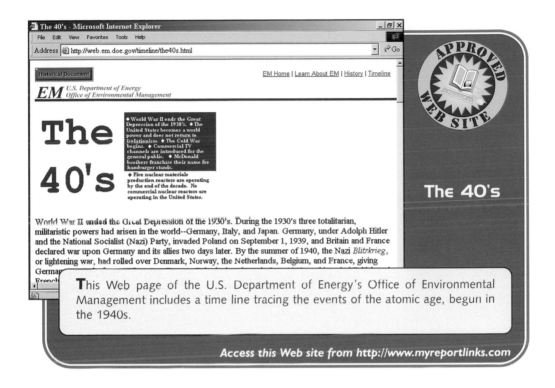

The 40's - Microsoft Internet Explorer

File Edit View Favorites Tools Help

Address http://web.em.doe.gov/timeline/the40s.html

EM Home | Learn About EM | History | Timeline

Historical Document

EM U.S. Department of Energy
Office of Environmental Management

The 40's

◆ World War II ends the Great Depression of the 1930's. ◆ The United States becomes a world power and does not return to isolationism. ◆ The Cold War begins. ◆ Commercial TV channels are introduced for the general public. ◆ McDonald brothers franchise their name for hamburger stands.

◆ Five nuclear materials production reactors are operating by the end of the decade. No commercial nuclear reactors are operating in the United States.

The 40's

World War II ended the Great Depression of the 1930's. During the 1930's three totalitarian, militaristic powers had arisen in the world—Germany, Italy, and Japan. Germany, under Adolph Hitler and the National Socialist (Nazi) Party, invaded Poland on September 1, 1939, and Britain and France declared war upon Germany and its allies two days later. By the summer of 1940, the Nazi *Blitzkrieg*, or lightening war, had rolled over Denmark, Norway, the Netherlands, Belgium, and France, giving Germa...

French...

This Web page of the U.S. Department of Energy's Office of Environmental Management includes a time line tracing the events of the atomic age, begun in the 1940s.

Access this Web site from http://www.myreportlinks.com

no jobs, or jobs which were wholly inadequate. And through them, I began to understand how deeply political and economic events could affect men's lives. I began to feel the need to participate more fully in the life of the community."[13]

Although it is nearly impossible to know whether Oppenheimer ever joined the American Communist party, he did attend its meetings and contributed money to its causes, such as the Spanish Civil War. Many progressive Americans participated in the Communist party at this time in history, but it was a fact that would come back to haunt Oppenheimer and hurt him later in his career during the anti-Communist climate of the

1950s. When Oppenheimer's enemies tried to destroy his reputation in the 1950s, they accused him of treason, pointing to his Communist party sympathies as a way of saying he was disloyal to the United States. All evidence has since shown that Robert Oppenheimer was always loyal to his country and never gave secrets to the Soviet Union or any Communist party members.

In 1940, Oppenheimer married Katherine Puening, who, with her previous husband, had joined the Communist party. The Oppenheimers had two children: Peter, born in 1941, and Katherine, born in 1944.

DEFENDING THE UNITED STATES

On December 7, 1941, the United States fleet at Pearl Harbor, Hawaii, was attacked by Japan, bringing America into World War II on the side of the English, French, and Soviets. Within days, Germany declared war on the United States. Now the German threat of an atomic attack on the United States had become even more real. And now Oppenheimer's brilliance as a physicist would allow him to serve his country with distinction as the man who was behind the building of the atomic bomb.

OPPENHEIMER AND THE MANHATTAN PROJECT

The first three decades of the twentieth century saw a revolution in the science of physics unlike anything since Sir Isaac Newton's discoveries in the seventeenth century. Newton's model of the universe explains how things operate on the macro, or large scale, level of everyday life, such as the actions and reactions, for example, that happen when one pool ball collides with another.

But twentieth-century physicists found that Newton's theories failed to explain what happened in the micro, or very small scale, world of the atom. Try as they would, they could not get their experiments to come out right when applying classical Newtonian physics to the behavior of atoms.

As a result, physicists had to develop a whole new branch of physics called quantum mechanics, which used mathematics to carefully describe and predict the behavior of atoms and their subatomic particles. It is this twentieth-century scientific revolution in

CHAPTER 3

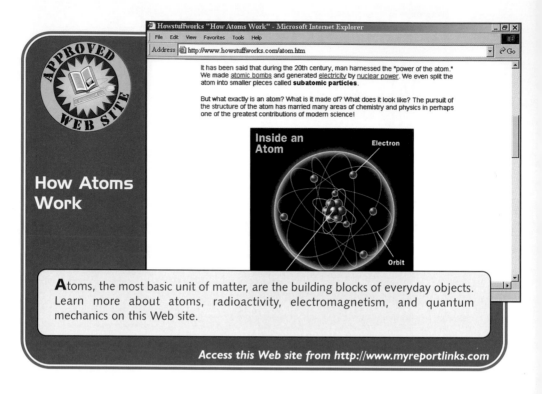

It has been said that during the 20th century, man harnessed the "power of the atom." We made atomic bombs and generated electricity by nuclear power. We even split the atom into smaller pieces called **subatomic particles**.

But what exactly is an atom? What is it made of? What does it look like? The pursuit of the structure of the atom has married many areas of chemistry and physics in perhaps one of the greatest contributions of modern science!

Inside an Atom

Electron

Orbit

How Atoms Work

Atoms, the most basic unit of matter, are the building blocks of everyday objects. Learn more about atoms, radioactivity, electromagnetism, and quantum mechanics on this Web site.

Access this Web site from http://www.myreportlinks.com

which Robert Oppenheimer participated that made the atomic bomb possible.

⊘ DEFINING THE STRUCTURE OF THE ATOM IN THE TWENTIETH CENTURY

The word *atom* comes from the Greek *atomos* and means "indivisible." The ancient Greeks defined *atom* as "the tiniest unit of matter beyond which nothing could be broken down further." The atomic bomb scientists were to prove this assumption false by dividing the atom and releasing the energy stored inside it.

But to divide the atom, the scientists had to first know what the atom looked like and how its particles behaved. The pioneering work of several physicists led to an accurate picture of the atom by the mid-1920s.

In 1897, J. J. Thomson discovered the electron, proving correctly that the atom was not the smallest unit of matter, but that all atoms were made up of subatomic particles. He proposed the initial model for the modern atom, nicknamed Thomson's pudding, saying that all atoms were spheres full of an electrically positive substance, with negative electrons inside like raisins stuck in a lump of pudding. His model for the atom was interesting, but it was wrong.

In 1912, Ernest Rutherford discovered the atomic nucleus. He found that most of the mass of the atom existed in its nucleus, and most of the rest

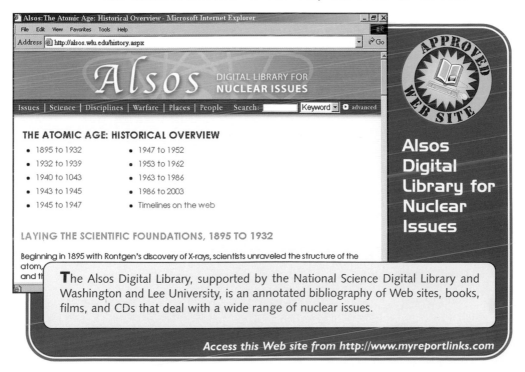

The Alsos Digital Library, supported by the National Science Digital Library and Washington and Lee University, is an annotated bibliography of Web sites, books, films, and CDs that deal with a wide range of nuclear issues.

Access this Web site from http://www.myreportlinks.com

of the atom was empty space in which negatively charged electrons moved. These electrons, he thought, spun around the nucleus like planets around the sun. This was called the atomic planetary model, which got closer to the truth but was overly simple and also incorrect.

In 1913, Niels Bohr, a Danish scientist who was to become Oppenheimer's friend, teacher, and mentor, created a new model of the atom. In Bohr's understanding of an atom, the orbits of the electrons were strictly defined, and electrons could exist at one energy level or orbit or another, but never in between. This sounds impossible, but the laws of nature at the subatomic level do not work like those in the macro world that we know so well. This was called the Bohr model.

In 1932, James Chadwick discovered that the nuclei of atoms consisted of positively charged protons as well as neutrons lacking any charge. This completed the basic structural model for the atom. However, there was no accurate model that explained how the three subatomic particles—electrons, protons, and neutrons—behaved and interacted with each other.

THE BIRTH OF QUANTUM MECHANICS

From 1905 to the mid-1930s, Albert Einstein, Max Planck, Niels Bohr, Erwin Schrödinger, Werner Heisenberg, and Max Born, one of Oppenheimer's teachers at Göttingen, developed a new theory of

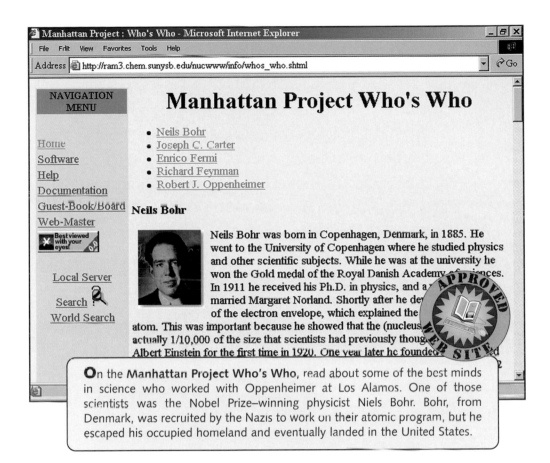

Manhattan Project Who's Who

NAVIGATION MENU

Home
Software
Help
Documentation
Guest-Book/Board
Web-Master

Local Server
Search
World Search

- Neils Bohr
- Joseph C. Carter
- Enrico Fermi
- Richard Feynman
- Robert J. Oppenheimer

Neils Bohr

Neils Bohr was born in Copenhagen, Denmark, in 1885. He went to the University of Copenhagen where he studied physics and other scientific subjects. While he was at the university he won the Gold medal of the Royal Danish Academy of Sciences. In 1911 he received his Ph.D. in physics, and a married Margaret Norland. Shortly after he de of the electron envelope, which explained the atom. This was important because he showed that the (nucleus) actually 1/10,000 of the size that scientists had previously thoug Albert Einstein for the first time in 1920. One year later he founded

On the **Manhattan Project Who's Who**, read about some of the best minds in science who worked with Oppenheimer at Los Alamos. One of those scientists was the Nobel Prize–winning physicist Niels Bohr. Bohr, from Denmark, was recruited by the Nazis to work on their atomic program, but he escaped his occupied homeland and eventually landed in the United States.

how atoms behave called quantum mechanics. With their theory, they turned classical Newtonian physics upside down.

The theoretical physicists used mathematics to find out how atoms and subatomic particles perform. They discovered to their amazement that matter and energy can be transformed into each other, or are equivalent. They also found that at the subatomic level, both matter and energy not only appear to exist as points (like billiard balls) but also have the characteristics of waves (like the up-and-down motion of the ocean), which seemed impossible. Einstein tried to resolve this paradox for decades but failed to do so, saying in 1924, "There are therefore now two theories of light, both indispensable, and—as one must admit today despite twenty years of tremendous effort on the part of theoretical physicists—without any logical connection."[1]

The discoverers of quantum mechanics learned that the subatomic universe is a very strange place, where matter can be converted into energy, and

Digital archival materials, including this photograph of Albert Einstein, left, and Leo Szilard, are provided on **The Manhattan Project: An Interactive History** Web site. The two scientists who wrote to President Franklin Roosevelt to warn him of Germany's atomic bomb program posed later for this picture.

energy into matter. Rutherford's neat planetary model of the atom was turned into a model in which electrons "spun" around the atom in a blur, or cloud, and in this spinning, their locations could never be truly known.

As strange as the rules of quantum mechanics seem, the mathematics of theoretical physics was found to apply beautifully to subatomic reality. Because of the knowledge gained by these pioneering physicists in quantum mechanics, the atomic bomb could now be built.

⊘ MEETING THE NAZI THREAT

On October 11, 1939, economist Alexander Sachs carried a letter to his friend, President Franklin Roosevelt, in the White House. It was one of the most important letters of the twentieth century. The correspondence came from physicists Albert Einstein and Leo Szilard, and it warned the president that the Nazis under Adolf Hitler were trying to build atomic "bombs of hitherto unenvisaged [unimagined] potency and scope."[2] The letter advised the president that the United States should hurry to develop its own atomic bomb to counter the Nazi threat.

Roosevelt responded to this startling news by asking bluntly, "Alex, what you are after is to see that the Nazis don't blow us up?"

"Precisely," said Sachs.[3]

Roosevelt immediately ordered the start of a program to beat the Germans in the development of the first atomic bomb. At first, the program lacked adequate leadership and got off to a very slow start. Meanwhile, the Nazis moved ahead, banning the export of uranium from any of the uranium mines in their territories, since the atomic bomb could not be built without it. They also went on to try to develop several atomic piles, an early form of nuclear reactor designed to create a sustained fission reaction. In such a reaction, the nucleus of an atom is split in two, creating two new nuclei and releasing large amounts of energy. An atomic pile releases energy slowly, while an atomic bomb releases the energy very quickly. In 1940, the Americans were still far from developing their own atomic pile or a bomb.

⇒ EARLY DEVELOPMENTS

America's atom bomb scientists knew that to create an atomic bomb, a fission chain reaction must be quickly set in motion. In this chain reaction, one fast-moving neutron collides with the nucleus of an atom, which is broken apart into two nuclei while also releasing several more fast-moving neutrons and lots of energy. Those fast-moving neutrons then do the same thing: breaking more nuclei apart, releasing more neutrons and more and more energy. All of this happens in less than a

▲ On December 2, 1942, the world's first controlled nuclear chain reaction took place on the campus of the University of Chicago. The reactor, named *Chicago Pile Number One*, was built by the renowned physicist Enrico Fermi (bottom row, left) and his colleagues, known as the *Chicago Pile Team*.

second, causing a massive explosion as all of the nuclear energy is released at once.

The scientists also knew that unstable radioactive elements could best be used to make such a bomb. They theorized that uranium 235, an unstable isotope of uranium 238, as well as plutonium, an entirely new element, could be used for the bomb. Plutonium was an element thought to exist but not discovered until early in 1941.

➲ How Much Uranium?

What no one knew is how much uranium it would take to make a bomb. Was it a pound, ten pounds, a hundred pounds, or more? On October 21, 1941, J. Robert Oppenheimer joined the top secret Uranium Committee formed by President Roosevelt. As part of the committee, Oppenheimer calculated exactly how much U-235 would be needed to make the first atomic bomb. The amount was called the critical mass. Critical mass was the amount of radioactive bomb material needed to cause a sudden chain reaction resulting in an atomic explosion. Thanks to Oppenheimer's thorough and precise calculations, his cooperation quickly became invaluable to the Uranium Committee. Suddenly, Oppenheimer saw a way that he could do his patriotic duty and defend America from the Nazis. He committed himself to doing all he could to help build the atomic bomb.

Soon, scientists from universities across the United States were recruited to work on the atomic bomb project, which was eventually given the code name the Manhattan Project. Oppenheimer remained at Berkeley, working on what was called "fast-neutron" research. He and his fellow professors and graduate students offered invaluable assistance in determining how an atomic bomb might be built.

But a problem developed. The American atomic bomb program was moving very slowly and was in danger of falling behind the Nazi program because there was no central scientific authority

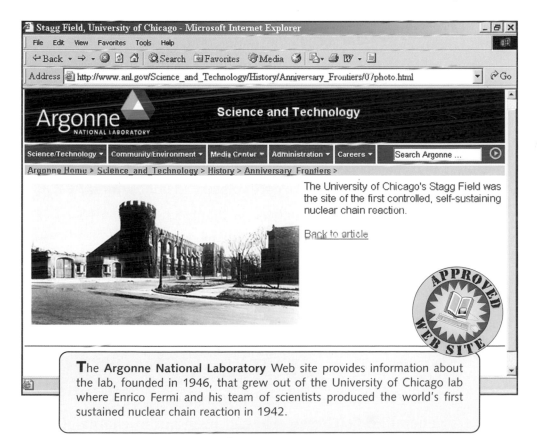

Stagg Field, University of Chicago - Microsoft Internet Explorer

File   Edit   View   Favorites   Tools   Help

Back ▾ → ▾ 🖉 🖉 🖄 | 🔍Search 🖆Favorites 🖆Media 🖆 | 🖆▾ 🖆 🖫 ▾ 🖹

Address 🖉 http://www.anl.gov/Science_and_Technology/History/Anniversary_Frontiers/0/photo.html   ▾   🖉 Go

Argonne
NATIONAL LABORATORY

Science and Technology

Science/Technology ▾ | Community/Environment ▾ | Media Center ▾ | Administration ▾ | Careers ▾ | Search Argonne ... | ▶

Argonne Home > Science_and_Technology > History > Anniversary Frontiers >

The University of Chicago's Stagg Field was the site of the first controlled, self-sustaining nuclear chain reaction.

Back to article

The Argonne National Laboratory Web site provides information about the lab, founded in 1946, that grew out of the University of Chicago lab where Enrico Fermi and his team of scientists produced the world's first sustained nuclear chain reaction in 1942.

running the project. As a result, universities around the country were unaware of what other universities were doing, and they often duplicated each other's work, wasting time. Oppenheimer tried to solve this problem by getting together some of the top theoretical physicists in the United States in the summer of 1942 for a secret symposium to discuss the atomic bomb.

The scientists at the symposium began their work by studying one of the biggest human-made explosions ever: an ammunition ship loaded with 5,000 tons of dynamite that had accidentally exploded in Halifax, Nova Scotia, in 1917. That explosion killed four thousand people and devastated two and a half square miles of the city. The physicists calculated that an atomic bomb could be built that would explode with a force two to three times that of the explosion in Halifax. They determined that a very compact atomic bomb could be built with a uranium core placed inside a metal sphere only eight inches in diameter. They also decided that the bomb would be very expensive, since the pure U-235 or pure plutonium used in the bomb did not exist in the natural world and would have to be manufactured in secret, in huge factories.

THE SECRET CITY IN THE DESERT

These things became the problem of U.S. Army general Leslie Groves. He had been put in charge

General Leslie Groves chose J. Robert Oppenheimer to head the laboratory at Los Alamos. The two men, though of very different temperaments and backgrounds, respected each other.

of the United States atomic bomb program known as the Manhattan Project on September 16, 1942. He was touring the country by train to visit all of the universities involved in the project, and he discovered to his dismay that the project was stalled amid much confusion. No one had yet been named to coordinate the research of the thousands of scientists involved in the project, to link the many threads of their research.

General Groves was determined to find one scientist, a natural leader, to guide the program. On October 15, 1942, Groves decided that he had found that man. He appointed Dr. J. Robert Oppenheimer as the Manhattan Project's scientific director, and he gave Oppenheimer his first big assignment: Find an ideal central location where the scientists now scattered around the country could be brought together to work on the building of the atomic bomb.

Oppenheimer went to work immediately. His first major task was to find a headquarters for the Manhattan Project. He chose Los Alamos, New Mexico. It was in the mountainous desert region where he had vacationed and ridden horses with his brother, Frank, since they were children.

While this remote, unpopulated region would be perfect for maintaining the Manhattan Project's secrecy, it was hardly ideal for a modern research laboratory. Oppenheimer's site housed the Los Alamos Ranch School, an 800-acre campus that included a main lodge, a dormitory, and a few

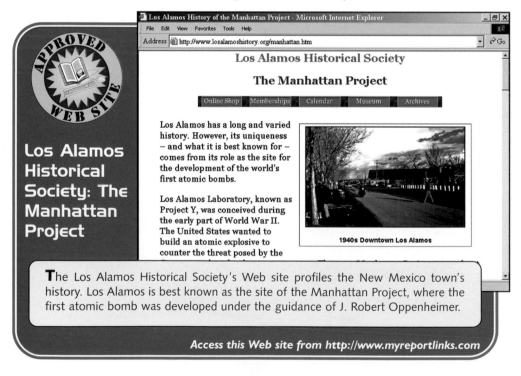

Los Alamos Historical Society: The Manhattan Project

Los Alamos History of the Manhattan Project - Microsoft Internet Explorer

File   Edit   View   Favorites   Tools   Help

Address http://www.losalamoshistory.org/manhattan.htm

Los Alamos Historical Society

The Manhattan Project

Online Shop   Memberships   Calendar   Museum   Archives

Los Alamos has a long and varied history. However, its uniqueness – and what it is best known for – comes from its role as the site for the development of the world's first atomic bombs.

Los Alamos Laboratory, known as Project Y, was conceived during the early part of World War II. The United States wanted to build an atomic explosive to counter the threat posed by the

1940s Downtown Los Alamos

The Los Alamos Historical Society's Web site profiles the New Mexico town's history. Los Alamos is best known as the site of the Manhattan Project, where the first atomic bomb was developed under the guidance of J. Robert Oppenheimer.

Access this Web site from http://www.myreportlinks.com

other small buildings. What he would need to build there was an entire city where thousands of scientists and their families could work and live. This city would not only need to include sophisticated scientific laboratories and machine shops of a sort never built before, but also everything else a normal city possessed: homes, a school, library, laundry, hospital, grocery stores, even a low-power radio station, and a recreation center. Amazingly, this secret city was built in a few short months in the beginning of 1943.

By the middle of 1945, when the first bomb was exploded, Los Alamos had become a city of four thousand civilians and two thousand military men and women, living in three hundred apartment buildings and fifty-two dormitories. The top scientists each had their own home. The technical area consisted of thirty-seven buildings, including a plutonium purification plant, a foundry, and dozens of individual research labs, plus warehouses and offices. All were surrounded by a ten-foot-high security fence and guarded by squads of military police.

⇒ THE "MAYOR" OF LOS ALAMOS

J. Robert Oppenheimer had been accustomed to managing a small group of students at Berkeley. When he became scientific director at Los Alamos in the spring of 1943, he found himself in charge of thousands of people and nearly as many

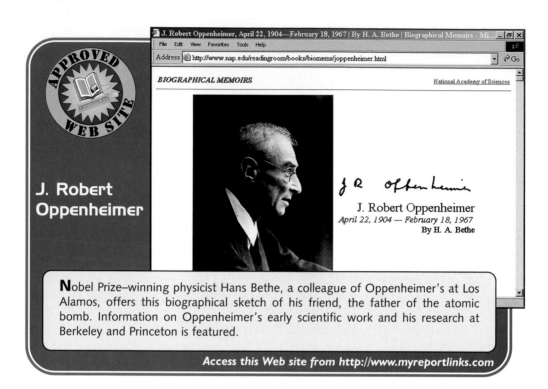

J. Robert Oppenheimer

BIOGRAPHICAL MEMOIRS

National Academy of Sciences

J. Robert Oppenheimer
April 22, 1904 — February 18, 1967
By H. A. Bethe

Nobel Prize–winning physicist Hans Bethe, a colleague of Oppenheimer's at Los Alamos, offers this biographical sketch of his friend, the father of the atomic bomb. Information on Oppenheimer's early scientific work and his research at Berkeley and Princeton is featured.

Access this Web site from http://www.myreportlinks.com

details. He not only had to finish building the secret city and equip its laboratory, but he also had to travel across America, recruiting just the right mix of scientists to work there. It was a task that exhausted him but one at which he succeeded brilliantly.

Oppenheimer populated his secret city at Los Alamos with some of the finest scientists on the planet: Enrico Fermi, Edward Teller, Hans Bethe, and Richard Feynman. There, for the next two years, these brilliant men and others worked long hours to solve the theoretical and technical problems involved in making the bomb. Throughout the project, Oppenheimer served as their undisputed leader.

The Uranium Bomb Problem

At Los Alamos, Oppenheimer not only brought together the nation's best theoretical and experimental physicists, but he also employed the talents of chemists, metallurgists, bomb ordnance experts, and machinists. They all set to work as a team to beat the Nazis and build the first atomic bomb, which they nicknamed "the gadget."

"The object of the project," wrote physicist Robert Serber, "is to produce a practical military weapon in the form of a bomb in which the energy is released by a fast neutron chain reaction in one or more of the materials known to show nuclear fission."[4]

There were two major challenges to making the bomb. First, there was hardly any pure fissionable material—U-235 or plutonium—in existence in the world from which the scientists could make a bomb. This problem was taken on at two other secret cities, Hanford, Washington, and Oak Ridge, Tennessee. The uranium bomb would ultimately require a cantaloupe-sized piece of U-235 weighing in at about thirty-three pounds (fifteen kilograms). The plutonium bomb needed less critical mass, so the plutonium required had to be no bigger than an apple and weigh about eleven pounds (five kilograms). Still, it would take nearly two years to

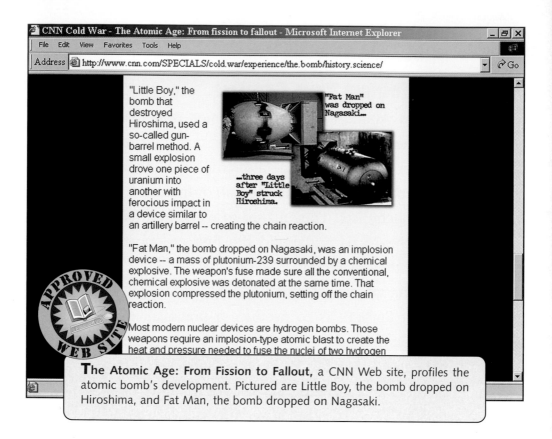

CNN Cold War - The Atomic Age: From fission to fallout - Microsoft Internet Explorer

File   Edit   View   Favorites   Tools   Help

Address   http://www.cnn.com/SPECIALS/cold.war/experience/the.bomb/history.science/

"Little Boy," the bomb that destroyed Hiroshima, used a so-called gun-barrel method. A small explosion drove one piece of uranium into another with ferocious impact in a device similar to an artillery barrel -- creating the chain reaction.

"Fat Man" was dropped on Nagasaki...

...three days after "Little Boy" struck Hiroshima.

"Fat Man," the bomb dropped on Nagasaki, was an implosion device -- a mass of plutonium-239 surrounded by a chemical explosive. The weapon's fuse made sure all the conventional, chemical explosive was detonated at the same time. That explosion compressed the plutonium, setting off the chain reaction.

Most modern nuclear devices are hydrogen bombs. Those weapons require an implosion-type atomic blast to create the heat and pressure needed to fuse the nuclei of two hydrogen

The Atomic Age: From Fission to Fallout, a CNN Web site, profiles the atomic bomb's development. Pictured are Little Boy, the bomb dropped on Hiroshima, and Fat Man, the bomb dropped on Nagasaki.

produce that small amount of fissionable material.

The second problem faced by the atomic bomb scientists was the one that Oppenheimer needed to solve: What mechanism would make the bomb work? The theoretical physicists understood how much fissionable material they would need to make a U-235 or plutonium bomb, but they did not know what it would look like or how it would operate.

The basic problem with both bombs was the same: how to bring together a critical mass of fissionable uranium or plutonium in just the right

K 6

J. R. Oppenheimer

▲ Security badges were issued to all employees of the Manhattan Project, including J. Robert Oppenheimer. Only the scientists involved in the project actually knew what they were working on at Los Alamos. Administrative people and technicians, as well as the wives of many employees, were kept in the dark about the nature of the work being done there.

proportions to create a high-speed chain reaction and sudden detonation as a powerful bomb.

→ A Solution Is Found

Scientists wrestling with the construction of the uranium atomic bomb worked day and night, six days a week, and they came up with a solution in the form of what they called a uranium gun. The uranium bomb they built was known as "Little Boy" because it was sleeker than the plutonium bomb. It was a long cylinder with a rounded nose and stabilizing fins at the back. Inside the cylinder was a modified artillery piece. A small explosive charge would propel a small piece of uranium down the "gun barrel" into a second subcritical piece of uranium, a piece too small to keep a chain reaction going. When the two pieces came together, they would have the required critical mass to cause an atomic bomb detonation. Neutrons would begin colliding with nuclei again and again, leading to a kind of explosion never made by human beings before.

Some of the scientists believed that this kind of explosion could be powerful enough to actually light the earth's atmosphere on fire and destroy the planet. Since they calculated less than a one-in-a-million chance of the bomb actually destroying the earth's atmosphere, the scientists decided to continue their work. They put the finishing touches on the uranium bomb by the spring of 1945.

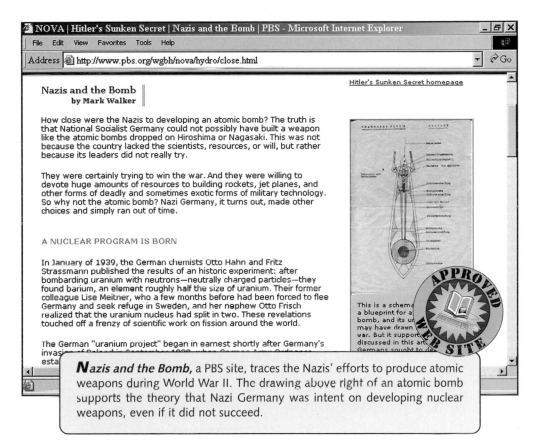

NOVA | Hitler's Sunken Secret | Nazis and the Bomb | PBS - Microsoft Internet Explorer

File   Edit   View   Favorites   Tools   Help

Address   http://www.pbs.org/wgbh/nova/hydro/close.html   Go

Hitler's Sunken Secret homepage

Nazis and the Bomb
by Mark Walker

How close were the Nazis to developing an atomic bomb? The truth is that National Socialist Germany could not possibly have built a weapon like the atomic bombs dropped on Hiroshima or Nagasaki. This was not because the country lacked the scientists, resources, or will, but rather because its leaders did not really try.

They were certainly trying to win the war. And they were willing to devote huge amounts of resources to building rockets, jet planes, and other forms of deadly and sometimes exotic forms of military technology. So why not the atomic bomb? Nazi Germany, it turns out, made other choices and simply ran out of time.

A NUCLEAR PROGRAM IS BORN

In January of 1939, the German chemists Otto Hahn and Fritz Strassmann published the results of an historic experiment: after bombarding uranium with neutrons—neutrally charged particles—they found barium, an element roughly half the size of uranium. Their former colleague Lise Meitner, who a few months before had been forced to flee Germany and seek refuge in Sweden, and her nephew Otto Frisch realized that the uranium nucleus had split in two. These revelations touched off a frenzy of scientific work on fission around the world.

The German "uranium project" began in earnest shortly after Germany's invasion of Poland in September 1939, when German Army Ordnance esta

This is a schema a blueprint for a bomb, and its u may have drawn war. But it suppor discussed in this ar Germans sought to

Nazis and the Bomb, a PBS site, traces the Nazis' efforts to produce atomic weapons during World War II. The drawing above right of an atomic bomb supports the theory that Nazi Germany was intent on developing nuclear weapons, even if it did not succeed.

THE PLUTONIUM BOMB PROBLEM

Scientists at Los Alamos hoped that the gun approach could also be used to make a plutonium bomb. By April 15, 1943, however, they found that a gun device would make the explosion uneven, which could threaten the bomb's success.

A different method had to be found to create the needed critical mass in the plutonium bomb. After many failed attempts and tests, the plutonium bomb, dubbed "Fat Man," was the result.

Instead of a gun, this bomb used an implosion method to compress a loose noncritical mass of fissionable plutonium into a tight critical mass of fissionable plutonium.

Fat Man was shaped something like a bulging watermelon with stabilizing fins at one end. It worked when explosive charges at the outside edge of the bomb were focused inward through what was called an implosion lens. These explosions sent a shock wave toward the center of the bomb, forcing the fissionable plutonium material together tighter and tighter. When the plutonium hit critical mass, neutrons would begin splitting plutonium atoms at a sudden fast rate, creating a chain reaction and huge explosion.

The plutonium bomb was ready for use by the summer of 1944, but because it was so complex, no one was sure it would work. Oppenheimer and the other physicists thought the plutonium bomb should be tested before it was used against a military target.

⊜ THE SURRENDER OF GERMANY

The atomic bomb, built to use against Nazi Germany, would never be used against Hitler or his people. Adolf Hitler committed suicide on April 30, 1945, and by May 7, World War II in Europe came to an end with Germany's signed surrender to the Allies (although the German command was not ordered to cease military activities until May 8). Suddenly, the race to build an atomic bomb before Germany could was over. In his memoirs, Emilio Segrè, a physicist who had worked on the

Manhattan Project at Los Alamos, recalled, "Now that the bomb could not be used against the Nazis, doubts arose," referring to whether or not to continue building it. As he revealed, "Those doubts, even if they do not appear in official reports, were discussed in many private discussions."[5]

Leo Szilard, who with Albert Einstein had written the 1939 letter to Franklin Roosevelt, became very worried. With the war against Germany over, the physicist felt certain that the new atomic bomb would be used against the Japanese and reveal America's nuclear weapons secret to the world.

No one who saw it could forget it, a foul and

Trinity Remembered is a commemorative site that provides photographs, maps, historical documents, and eyewitness accounts of the Trinity test, the first test of a nuclear weapon.

EDITOR'S CHOICE

With that secret revealed, Szilard was sure that the United States and the Soviet Union would begin a fierce nuclear arms race, which had the potential of ending in nuclear war and destroying the earth. After Germany's surrender, Szilard circulated a petition, signed by some of his fellow scientists at Los Alamos, urging the United States not to use the bomb against Japan. But the petition was not able to change the mind of President Harry S Truman, who had succeeded to the presidency following Franklin Roosevelt's death on April 12. With the war in the Pacific continuing and Japanese fighters engaging in desperate attacks on American troops, Truman went ahead with plans to use the atomic bomb on the Japanese.

→ THE TRINITY TEST

The last major undertaking of the scientists at Los Alamos was a test of the plutonium bomb. That test was carried out on July 16, 1945. Brigadier General Thomas Farrell described what Oppenheimer and the other scientists from Los Alamos saw that day at the Trinity test in the New Mexico desert.

> No man-made phenomenon of such tremendous power had ever occurred before. The lighting effects beggared description. The whole country was lighted by a searing light with the intensity many times that of the midday sun. . . . It lighted every peak, crevasse and ridge of the nearby mountain

range with a clarity and beauty that cannot be described but must be seen to be imagined. It was that beauty the great poets dream about but describe most poorly and inadequately. Thirty seconds after the explosion came, first, the air blast pressing hard against people and things, to be followed almost immediately by the strong, sustained, awesome roar which warned of doomsday and made us feel that we puny things were blasphemous to dare tamper with the forces heretofore reserved to the Almighty.[6]

The Trinity test atomic bomb exploded with the force of 18,600 tons of dynamite. Scientists at

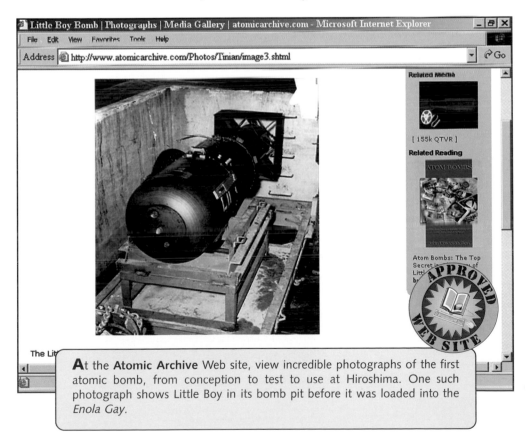

Little Boy Bomb | Photographs | Media Gallery | atomicarchive.com - Microsoft Internet Explorer

File   Edit   View   Favorites   Tools   Help

Address http://www.atomicarchive.com/Photos/Tinian/image3.shtml

Related Media

[155k QTVR]

Related Reading

Atom Bombs: The Top Secret...of Little...by

APPROVED WEB SITE

At the **Atomic Archive** Web site, view incredible photographs of the first atomic bomb, from conception to test to use at Hiroshima. One such photograph shows Little Boy in its bomb pit before it was loaded into the *Enola Gay.*

Los Alamos cheered and hugged, congratulating each other. The shock wave from the bomb broke windows 120 miles away and was felt by many people at least 160 miles away. The United States Army falsely reported that an ammunition dump had accidentally exploded at the Alamogordo Bombing Range.

Meanwhile, at about the same moment that J. Robert Oppenheimer was watching the successful test of the plutonium bomb in the New Mexico desert, a ship was being loaded in San Francisco Bay with the pieces of a uranium atomic bomb. In the floodlit morning of July 16, 1945, the crew of the USS *Indianapolis* loaded the triggering mechanism for the Little Boy atomic bomb onto the deck of their ship. Within hours, the *Indianapolis* would sail for the island of Tinian in the Pacific Ocean. That small island became the staging ground for the first atomic bomb attack ever in the history of warfare.

LIFE AFTER THE ATOMIC BOMB

Many new inventions require years or even decades to be recognized and accepted as useful by people. That was not the case with the atomic bomb. Within less than a month of the successful Trinity test, nuclear weapons would be used against two Japanese cities, killing hundreds of thousands of people.

After President Roosevelt died in office on April 12, 1945, his vice president, Harry Truman, replaced him as president and became the man who would decide if the atomic bomb should be used against Japan. On July 24, fearing that tens of thousands of American soldiers would die in an invasion of the Japanese islands, Truman approved the use of the atomic bomb on Japan. No "last chance" warning was to be given to the Japanese that the attack was coming. No demonstration of the bomb to the Japanese by dropping it on an uninhabited island or other desolate place was proposed. Instead the military order simply

CHAPTER

4

Nuclear
Files.org

Nuclear Files: Timeline of the Nuclear Age: 1945 - Microsoft Internet Explorer

File   Edit   View   Favorites   Tools   Help

Address http://www.nuclearfiles.org/menu/timeline/1940/1945.htm   Go

NUCLEAR Files.org
PROJECT OF THE NUCLEAR AGE PEACE FOUNDATION

| Home | Timeline | Key Issues | Library | Educators | About Us | Donate |

Timeline of the Nuclear Age → 1945   search

1945 - The Decision to Drop the Bomb

The decision to drop the atomic bombs on the cities of Hiroshima and Nagasaki is one of the most controversial issues of the 20th century. Many modern historians have criticized the commonly held perceptions that the bomb shortened the war, saved American lives and prevented USSR's sharing in the post-war administration of Japan (see, for example, *Hiroshima's Shadow* edited by Kai Bird & Lawrence Lifschultz). In 1995, on the 50th anniversary of the bombing, an exhibit designed to commemorate the event resulted in unprecedented controversy for the Smithsonian Institution. The American Legion and other veteran's organizations successfully lobbied against the inclusion of quotes from a number of notables including Dwight D. Eisenhower that questioned the necessity of the bomb's use.

The debate has not subsided. This timeline seeks to chronicle the events in 1945 leading up to and following the bombings. In 1945 the Manhattan Project, the ambitious and expensive US effort to create the atomic bomb, succeeded in its mission. The first atomic device was tested at Alamogordo, New Mexico on July 16, 1945. Three weeks later the atomic bomb was used on the

📧 E-mail this Page
🖨 Printer Friendly

1945

More on the Web →

▪ Albert Einstein Online
▪ Enrico Fermi
▪ Leo Szilard Online
▪ Harry S. Truman
▪ Minutes of the second

With this site, the Nuclear Age Peace Foundation and the National Science Digital Library present information about the history of the atomic age. Topics include the Manhattan Project, the Cuban Missile Crisis, nuclear weapons, and treaties concerning their use.

EDITOR'S CHOICE

Access this Web site from http://www.myreportlinks.com

read: "The 509th Composite Group, 20th Air Force, will deliver its first special bomb as soon as weather will permit visual bombing after about 3 August 1945, on one of the targets: Hiroshima, Kokura, Niigata and Nagasaki. . . ."[1] With that order, the fate of several hundred thousand Japanese people was decided.

⊖ HIROSHIMA

At about 2:30 in the morning of August 6, 1945, the *Enola Gay,* a B-29 Super Fortress bomber, rolled onto the runway of Tinian Island in the Pacific Ocean. In its bomb bay was the first atomic bomb that would be dropped on people. Shortly before the plane took off, a Protestant chaplain had prayed for the plane and its crew, asking God "to be with those who brave the heights of Thy heaven and who carry the battle to our enemies."[2] The plane taxied out to the runway, gained speed, and took off. Its destination was the Japanese city of Hiroshima.

Several hours later, the plane arrived above Hiroshima's Aioi Bridge where it crossed the Ota River at the heart of the city. The bombardier let the bomb go. The plane turned and raced away from the scene.

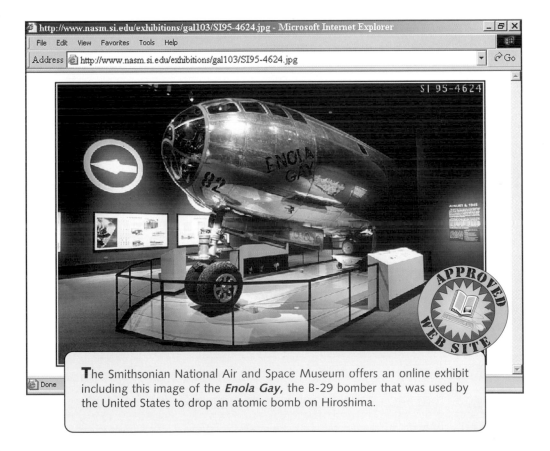

The Smithsonian National Air and Space Museum offers an online exhibit including this image of the *Enola Gay*, the B-29 bomber that was used by the United States to drop an atomic bomb on Hiroshima.

Little Boy, the U-235 atomic bomb, exploded at 8:16 A.M. Hiroshima time. An instant after the bomb detonated, the city that had lain below vanished beneath the atomic bomb's mushroom cloud. "Where we had seen a clear city two minutes before, we could now no longer see the city. We could see smoke and fires creeping up the sides of the mountains," said one of the crew.[3] Another crew member said that the entire city looked like "a pot of boiling black oil" while

▲ A panoramic photograph of Hiroshima taken by the U.S. Army from about a half mile away shows the utter devastation the atomic bomb caused.

another said it looked like the whole city had been covered in lava.[4] "It was all impersonal," pilot Paul Tibbets said of the mission and the scene below.[5] In an instant, much of the city of Hiroshima had ceased to exist, destroyed by the force of a single atomic bomb.

At the heart of the city where the bomb's temperature reached 5,400°F (2,982°C), no one survived. "People exposed within half a mile of the Little Boy fireball . . . were seared to bundles of smoking black char in a fraction of a second as their internal organs boiled away," wrote Richard Rhodes in his Pulitzer Prize–winning book *The Making of the Atomic Bomb*.[6] Charred bodies, scattered in the street, numbered in the thousands. More than nine tenths of the people within six tenths of a mile (965 meters) of where the bomb exploded died.

⊖"The Way War Really Looks"

Those who survived the bomb attack told horrendous stories later. A woman who was five years old at the time of the blast recalled, "People came fleeing from the nearby streets. One after another they were almost unrecognizable. The skin was burned off some of them and was hanging from their hands and from their chins; their faces were red and so swollen that you could hardly tell where their eyes and mouths were."[7]

A fifth-grade boy later offered a list of what he saw:

> The child making a suffering, groaning sound, his burned face swollen up balloon-like and jerking as he wanders among the fires. The old man, the skin of his face and body peeling off like a potato skin, mumbling prayers while he flees . . . Another man pressing with both hands the wound from which blood is steadily dripping, rushing around as though he has gone mad and calling the names of his wife and child—ah—my hair seems to stand on end just to remember. This is the way war really looks.[8]

⇒ RADIATION SICKNESS

The atomic bomb was like no weapon used before in history. For those who survived the initial blast, who were not blown up or burned and believed they had been spared, there was often the slow, painful death caused by radiation sickness. During and after the attack, their bodies had been pierced by gamma rays, high-energy rays composed of energetic photons, that destroyed their organs and tissues. Those with radiation sickness suffered nausea, vomiting, diarrhea, fever, and weakness. Purple spots appeared on the skin from internal bleeding. People bled from their mouth, throat, and other places. Their hair fell out. Their white blood cell count plummeted, and many died. The radiation from the bomb would also cause many more thousands to die of cancer and other diseases for several decades after the bomb blast.

⇒THE JAPANESE RESPONSE

The Japanese government was at first unable to respond to what had happened. One of Japan's cities had been swallowed up and destroyed on a single morning. Not only were thousands of people dead, but everything else was gone: homes, factories, hospitals, schools, police stations, courts, grocery stores, gas stations, radio stations, and military bases. Also gone were the ties of human society: whole neighborhoods and families, people's careers, pets, heirlooms, photo albums—everything was gone. At Hiroshima, the atomic bomb ripped the fabric of human society into shreds.

Although it is impossible to know how many people were killed immediately, it is estimated that 70,000 died in the blast or in its early aftermath. By the end of 1945, the death toll may have exceeded 100,000, and after five years' time, 200,000, from radiation sickness, cancer, or other diseases resulting from the bomb attack.

The United States was impatient for a response from the Japanese, but the Japanese could not respond quickly because of the confusion over what had happened at Hiroshima. With all of the city's communications knocked out by the bomb, a full day passed before people in Tokyo, Japan's

75

capital, even learned of the bombing. Despite the devastation of Hiroshima, the more militant members of the Japanese government refused to surrender.

NAGASAKI

On August 9, 1945, three days after the bombing of Hiroshima, a second atomic bomb was dropped on a Japanese city. The target this time was Nagasaki, a city on the western coast of the island of Kyushu. William L. Laurence, a reporter for the

▲ The Japanese city of Nagasaki, the second target of an atomic bomb, was reduced to a desolate landscape.

New York Times, went along for the ride and commented on what he saw as the plutonium bomb nicknamed Fat Man exploded over the city:

> It is a thing of beauty to behold, this "gadget." In its design went millions of man-hours of what is without a doubt the most concentrated intellectual effort in history. Never before had so much brain-power been focused on a single problem. . . .
>
> Observers in the tail of our ship [airplane] saw a giant ball of fire rise as though from the bowels of the earth, belching forth enormous white smoke rings. Next they saw a giant pillar of purple fire, 10,000 feet high, shooting skyward with enormous speed.
>
> By the time our ship had made another turn in the direction of the atomic explosion the pillar of purple fire had reached the level of our altitude. Only about 45 seconds had passed. Awe-struck, we watched it shoot upward like a meteor coming from the earth instead of from outer space, becoming ever more alive as it climbed skyward through the white clouds. It was no longer smoke, or dust, or even a cloud of fire. It was a living thing, a new species of being, born right before our incredulous eyes.[9]

The Nagasaki bombing mission went off without a hitch. The plutonium bomb proved to be just as successful as the U-235 bomb. By the end of 1945, seventy thousand people had died as a result of the bombing of Nagasaki. Over the next five years, seventy thousand more people died of radiation sickness or other bomb-related illnesses. As at Hiroshima, 54 percent of the population was killed. Ninety-five percent of those who died were not soldiers but civilians. On August 14, five days after the second bomb was dropped, the empire of Japan finally agreed to surrender, finally bringing an end to the Second World War. The American people and the scientists at Los Alamos celebrated that event.

THE POSTWAR ERA AND THE A-BOMB

When we think of inventions, we tend to think of

things that make life easier or better or more rewarding. In general, inventions are good for people. It is difficult, then, to find anything positive to say about the invention, or development, of the atomic bomb. Unlike most other inventions, its greatest benefit has come from its

◀ When Harry S Truman was Franklin Roosevelt's vice president, he was not even told of the top secret Manhattan Project. Once Truman succeeded Roosevelt as president, he was quickly brought up to speed and made the fateful decision to use atomic weapons to end World War II.

not being used. In the years after Hiroshima and Nagasaki, international politics and government policy were largely shaped by attempts to control the spread of nuclear weapons and by showdowns between nations to prevent their use.

Day-to-day life also changed as people dealt with the very real possibility that a nuclear war could begin at any moment—maybe even by accident—and end civilization in a matter of minutes. It is a threat we still live with today.

⇒ THE BOMB AND THE ARMS RACE

The complexities and cost of developing the first atomic bomb made many American politicians, such as President Harry Truman, think that only the United States would be capable of building and affording nuclear weapons. Physicists like Oppenheimer argued otherwise, saying that it would be relatively easy and inexpensive for other nations to develop their own bombs once the United States had shown that it could be done.

Oppenheimer and other physicists feared that the United States would not long hold a monopoly on the atomic bomb. Oppenheimer argued that the United Nations should control all nuclear weapons to prevent their proliferation, or spread, saying, "The safety of this nation, as opposed to its ability to inflict damage on an enemy power, cannot lie wholly or entirely in its scientific or technical

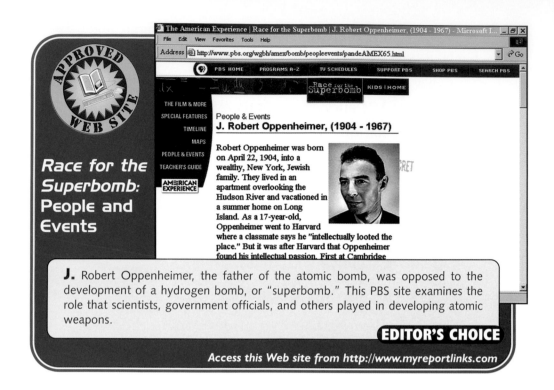

Race for the Superbomb: People and Events

J. Robert Oppenheimer, the father of the atomic bomb, was opposed to the development of a hydrogen bomb, or "superbomb." This PBS site examines the role that scientists, government officials, and others played in developing atomic weapons.

EDITOR'S CHOICE

Access this Web site from http://www.myreportlinks.com

prowess. It can only be based on making future wars impossible."[10]

Oppenheimer also opposed further nuclear bomb testing and the development of a hydrogen bomb, known as the superbomb. His fears were that if the United States moved forward with its plans, other nations would also do nuclear tests and build hydrogen bombs. There would be an all-out arms race, with each country trying to better protect itself with more numerous and more powerful nuclear weapons.

It turned out that Oppenheimer and the other physicists were right. Without UN control, other nations began to develop their own nuclear weapons and test them. On August 29, 1949, the Soviet Union exploded its own atomic bomb. This resulted in an intense arms race between the United States and the Soviet Union that lasted until the collapse of the Soviet Union in 1991.

The development of intercontinental ballistic missiles in 1957 meant that an atomic bomb could be launched by rockets from anywhere in the world and hit and destroy a city in a matter of minutes. The United Kingdom built its first atomic bomb in 1952, and France built its first in 1960. Since then, Israel, Pakistan, China, India, and North Korea have all developed their own atomic weapons.

A Stockpile of Weapons

According to the United Nations, by 1980 there were approximately forty thousand nuclear warheads stockpiled around the planet, adding up to thirteen thousand megatons of dynamite in explosive power. Many experts believed this was enough weaponry to bring about the extinction of the human race. But still the arms race continued, with trillions of dollars spent on making nuclear weapons.

The 1980s and 1990s saw some attempts at nuclear disarmament, but by 2006 it was estimated that there were still more than sixteen thousand nuclear weapons ready for use and another four-teen thousand in storage in the world. The United States has nearly 7,000 ready for action and 3,000 in storage, and Russia has about 8,500 ready to launch and 11,000 in storage. It is estimated that China has 400 nuclear weapons, France 350, Britain 200, Israel 200, India 95, and Pakistan 50.

Iran and North Korea, two of three countries, including Iraq, that President George W. Bush included in his "axis of evil," continue to engage in activities that defy international agreements concerning nuclear armaments. In October 2006, North Korea tested a nuclear weapon, and Iran continues to enrich uranium, which could be used to make an atomic bomb, despite a U.N. Security Council demand to stop.

⇒ THE A-BOMB'S IMPACT ON EVERYDAY LIFE

With the invention of the atomic bomb, the threat of being killed in warfare went from being relatively remote to being almost immediate and a daily possibility. With a nuclear war, rockets and planes could be sent aloft in a matter of minutes and thousands of cities destroyed along with their entire populations.

For children growing up in the late 1940s, the 1950s, and the 1960s, the atomic bomb was like the new bogeyman. These children learned to fear the atomic bomb at a young age. Children in the United States feared being bombed by the Russians, while Russian children feared being bombed by the United States.

Schools in the United States had regular "duck and cover" exercises to "prepare" for a nuclear attack. A teacher would pretend to see a flash of light, an imagined nuclear explosion, and the children then had to dive under their desks or leave the classroom and file into a dark hallway where they would kneel on the floor and pull their jackets over their heads to protect them from an exploding atomic bomb. Experts agreed that such actions would have offered little protection against conventional bombs, and virtually no protection against the searing heat, blast, and deadly radiation of a nuclear weapon. But still the United States government required such exercises.

During the 1950s, some families and communities built fallout shelters. These were bunkers built underground and stocked with food and water.

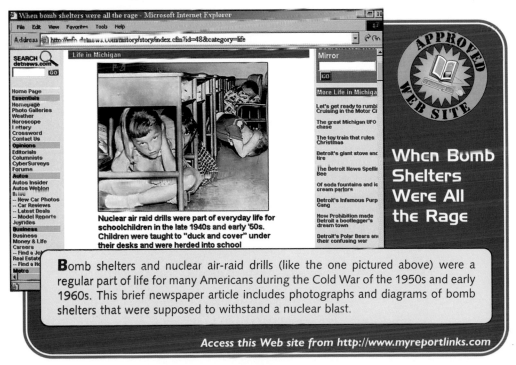

Nuclear air raid drills were part of everyday life for schoolchildren in the late 1940s and early '50s. Children were taught to "duck and cover" under their desks and were herded into school

Bomb shelters and nuclear air-raid drills (like the one pictured above) were a regular part of life for many Americans during the Cold War of the 1950s and early 1960s. This brief newspaper article includes photographs and diagrams of bomb shelters that were supposed to withstand a nuclear blast.

Access this Web site from http://www.myreportlinks.com

On March 5, 1946, J. Robert Oppenheimer, right, received the Presidential Medal of Merit from Secretary of War Robert B. Patterson. The award, at the time the highest honor a civilian could receive for service to his country, was created following World War II.

When an air-raid siren was heard, the family or community was supposed to gather inside the shelter and wait until the all-clear siren was sounded, meaning the nuclear attack was over. Most experts agreed that fallout shelters would have been useless against a direct hit by a nuclear bomb. Films produced by the American government, however, showed families surviving such attacks and then waiting a brief time to return to their homes. In reality, even if homes and neighborhoods somehow survived a nuclear bombing, the radiation from an atomic bomb attack would have made the community uninhabitable for months, years, or even decades afterward.

⊜ THE CUBAN MISSILE CRISIS

The authors of this book were seven and eleven years old, respectively, when the Soviet Union and the United States came close to engaging in a

http://www.gwu.edu/~nsarchiv/nsa/cuba_mis_cri/20.jpg - Microsoft Internet Explorer

File   Edit   View   Favorites   Tools   Help

Address   http://www.gwu.edu/~nsarchiv/nsa/cuba_mis_cri/20.jpg

Done

The Cuban Missile Crisis, 1962: The Fortieth Anniversary presents a collection of primary source materials from that pivotal event in American history. In this photograph taken at the White House, President John F. Kennedy, in rocker, speaks with Soviet Ambassador Anatoly Dobrynin, left, and Soviet Foreign Minster Andrei Gromyko. Kennedy did not reveal during this meeting that he already knew the Soviets had missiles in Cuba.

nuclear war over Soviet missile sites in Cuba. We both remember the autumn of 1962 as being a very frightening time in human history.

Early in October of that year, American spy planes flying over Cuba discovered that the Soviet Union was placing nuclear warheads and missiles there. That meant that such weapons would be less than a hundred miles from the United States mainland.

The people of the United States did not know about this threat until President John F. Kennedy went on television on October 22, 1962, to tell them about it. Showing aerial pictures of the missile sites, he spoke plainly about the seriousness of the situation.

> This Government, as promised, has maintained the closest surveillance of the Soviet military buildup on the island of Cuba. Within the past week, unmistakable evidence has established the fact that a series of offensive missile sites is now in

preparation on that imprisoned island. The purpose of these bases can be none other than to provide a nuclear strike capability against the Western Hemisphere.[11]

People across America watching television in their living rooms were struck by immediate fear and worry for their families. The president said that any nuclear missile attack from Cuba would be seen as an attack by the Soviet Union and would be met with an American nuclear attack on the Soviet Union and Cuba.

President Kennedy placed a naval quarantine, or blockade, on Cuba to prevent further Soviet shipments of military weapons from arriving there. United States military leaders wanted to attack the missile sites on the island right away. They were unaware that nuclear weapons in Cuba had already been armed and were ready to launch, and an attack on Cuba would have meant immediate nuclear war. Had American fighter

This spot in the desert landscape near Alamogordo, New Mexico, gives little indication that it was the place where the first nuclear weapon was detonated, more than sixty years ago.

planes attacked the Cuban missile sites, it could have been the start of World War III.

President Kennedy resisted attacking Cuba even after an American spy plane was shot down while photographing the missile sites. A Soviet fleet sailed toward the United States warships that formed the Cuban quarantine line. It looked as if the world was on the brink of nuclear war. In one classroom in New Jersey at the time when the Soviet and American ships were supposed to meet, a siren was heard, and the children feared that on that sunny October day their lives were about to come to an end. Fortunately, it was only a fire siren.

On October 28, the United States and Soviet Union reached a compromise. The Soviet ships turned back, and the nuclear missiles were removed from Cuba. In truth, the world had probably come within moments of nuclear war—a war that had become possible because of the development of the atomic bomb by J. Robert Oppenheimer and others in a southwestern desert some twenty years earlier.

FROM HERO TO VILLAIN

With the bombing of Hiroshima and Nagasaki in 1945, the atomic bomb was no longer a secret. In a very short time, J. Robert Oppenheimer went from being an obscure physicist, known only to his colleagues and students, to one of the most famous men on earth.

He was featured on the cover of *Time* magazine and interviewed by newspapers from around the world. Even his porkpie hat, which he wore everywhere, became legendary and was so easily recognized by everyone that it could be featured on the cover of *Physics Today* magazine, without Oppenheimer wearing it.

CHAPTER

5

The *New York Times* later described Oppenheimer's looming presence on the world stage from 1945 to 1952.

Dr. Oppenheimer's big-brimmed brown porkpie hat, size 6 7/8, was a frequent (and telltale) sight in Washington and the capitals of Western Europe, where he traveled to lecture or consult. . . . He was Oppy, Oppie or Opje to hundreds of persons who were captivated by his charm, eloquence and sharp, subtle humor and who were awed by the scope of his erudition [knowledge], the incisiveness of his mind, the chill of his sarcasm and his arrogance toward those he thought were slow or shoddy thinkers.[1]

Though thousands of people had worked on the atomic bomb, many playing important roles in its construction, Oppenheimer alone came to personify the new weapon. He became known as the father of the atomic bomb.

Nearly everyone in the United States—from the general public to the military and politicians—declared the forty-one-year-old scientist a hero. Many believed he had saved thousands of American soldiers' lives by developing the bomb dropped on Hiroshima and Nagasaki, because the planned invasion of Japan by American troops would have resulted in very high casualties. Since Japan had been America's enemy, few people gave deep thought to the hundreds of thousands of Japanese civilians killed by the bombs. As Secretary of War Henry L. Stimson declared, "The development of the bomb itself has been largely due to his [Oppenheimer's] genius and the inspiration and leadership he has given to his colleagues."[2]

A MAN OF PEACE

Though many people thought J. Robert Oppenheimer was a great hero in the first years

PHYSICS *today*

Robert Oppenheimer had become so famous following the end of World War II that something as simple as his porkpie hat became a signature piece, easily identified. Here it graces the May 1948 cover of *Physics Today*.

VOL 1 NO 1 ● MAY 1948

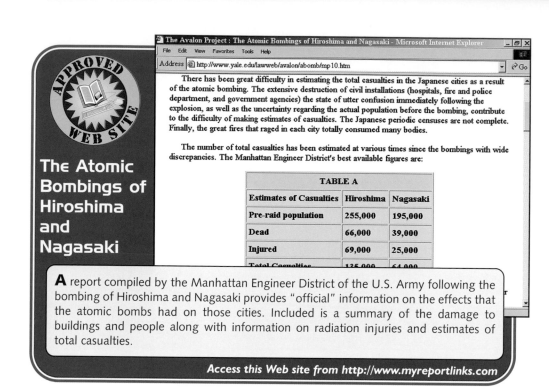

The Atomic Bombings of Hiroshima and Nagasaki

The Avalon Project : The Atomic Bombings of Hiroshima and Nagasaki - Microsoft Internet Explorer

File   Edit   View   Favorites   Tools   Help

Address   http://www.yale.edu/lawweb/avalon/abomb/mp10.htm   Go

There has been great difficulty in estimating the total casualties in the Japanese cities as a result of the atomic bombing. The extensive destruction of civil installations (hospitals, fire and police department, and government agencies) the state of utter confusion immediately following the explosion, as well as the uncertainty regarding the actual population before the bombing, contribute to the difficulty of making estimates of casualties. The Japanese periodic censuses are not complete. Finally, the great fires that raged in each city totally consumed many bodies.

The number of total casualties has been estimated at various times since the bombings with wide discrepancies. The Manhattan Engineer District's best available figures are:

TABLE A		
Estimates of Casualties	Hiroshima	Nagasaki
Pre-raid population	255,000	195,000
Dead	66,000	39,000
Injured	69,000	25,000
Total Casualties	135,000	64,000

A report compiled by the Manhattan Engineer District of the U.S. Army following the bombing of Hiroshima and Nagasaki provides "official" information on the effects that the atomic bombs had on those cities. Included is a summary of the damage to buildings and people along with information on radiation injuries and estimates of total casualties.

Access this Web site from http://www.myreportlinks.com

after the war, some began to change their opinions of him as time went on. They did not agree with his efforts toward peace and his support for the control of nuclear arms.

After the horrors of Hiroshima and Nagasaki, as the numbers of Japanese people killed became known, Oppenheimer became deeply disturbed. He also became convinced that a hydrogen bomb, which would be even more powerful than an atomic bomb, should not be developed, and that all of the world's countries should agree to manage their atomic energy programs together peacefully and openly.

In 1947, Oppenheimer firmly denounced the use of atomic weapons in future wars. He said that the dropping of the atomic bomb on Hiroshima and Nagasaki had "dramatized . . . mercilessly the inhumanity and evil of modern war." He also acknowledged guilt over what he and the other brilliant men of science with the Manhattan Project had accomplished: "In some sort of crude sense which no vulgarity, no humor, no overstatements can quite extinguish, the physicists have known sin; and this is a knowledge which they cannot lose."[3] Oppenheimer and some of the other physicists who had helped build the atomic bomb were critical of the United States continuing to work on a hydrogen bomb, fearing that a war in which such a weapon might be used would destroy all of humanity.

THE AEC

Oppenheimer failed in his efforts to prevent the development of the hydrogen bomb, to stop the proliferation of nuclear weapons, and to put all atomic energy research under the supervision of the United Nations. He did, however, succeed in getting all atomic research in the United States taken away from the military and put under the direction of a civilian agency, the Atomic Energy Commission (AEC). Oppenheimer served as the chair of a civilian advisory commission to the AEC from 1947 to 1952.

93

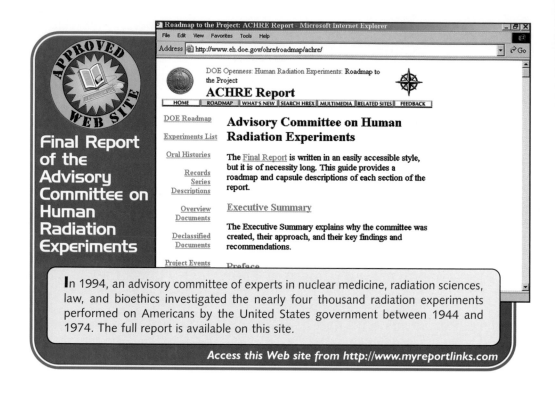

Final Report of the Advisory Committee on Human Radiation Experiments

Roadmap to the Project: ACHRE Report - Microsoft Internet Explorer

File   Edit   View   Favorites   Tools   Help

Address http://www.eh.doe.gov/ohre/roadmap/achre/   Go

DOE Openness: Human Radiation Experiments: Roadmap to the Project

ACHRE Report

HOME   ROADMAP   WHAT'S NEW   SEARCH HREX   MULTIMEDIA   RELATED SITES   FEEDBACK

DOE Roadmap

Experiments List

Oral Histories

Records Series Descriptions

Overview Documents

Declassified Documents

Project Events

Advisory Committee on Human Radiation Experiments

The Final Report is written in an easily accessible style, but it is of necessity long. This guide provides a roadmap and capsule descriptions of each section of the report.

Executive Summary

The Executive Summary explains why the committee was created, their approach, and their key findings and recommendations.

Preface

In 1994, an advisory committee of experts in nuclear medicine, radiation sciences, law, and bioethics investigated the nearly four thousand radiation experiments performed on Americans by the United States government between 1944 and 1974. The full report is available on this site.

Access this Web site from http://www.myreportlinks.com

Oppenheimer remained concerned about the proliferation of nuclear weapons for the rest of his life. Though he had worked tirelessly to develop the atomic bomb, he now worried that it would be used to destroy civilization. In a speech at Los Alamos, urging peaceful international cooperation on the development of nuclear energy, he said, "If atomic bombs are to be added to the arsenals of a warring world, or to the arsenals of nations preparing for war, then the time will come when mankind will curse the name of Los Alamos and Hiroshima. The peoples of this world must unite, or they will perish."[4]

➡ TRAITOR AND SPY?

Oppenheimer's strong arguments for peace ran counter to the mood of the nation during the early 1950s. Cold War tensions between the United States and the Soviet Union were heating up. Suspicions about Communists holding positions of power in American government, and fears that scientists would divulge nuclear secrets to the Soviets, led to government hearings in which many people were unfairly accused and their careers ruined as a result. Many people at that time, especially in the armed forces and in government, supported a strong military presence and large atomic arsenal to keep the country safe. They were afraid of giving over control of nuclear weapons to the United Nations. Oppenheimer's ideas on peace were unpopular even with American presidents Harry S Truman and Dwight D. Eisenhower.

In 1953, Oppenheimer was accused of being a traitor to the United States based on his sympathies toward pro-Communist groups and liberal causes during the 1930s. It was true that Oppenheimer had then been what was called a "fellow traveler," donating money to the American Communist party and sometimes attending its meetings and rallies. But there is no evidence that he ever officially joined the Communist party or supported an overthrow of the United States government.

Oppenheimer was not alone. Many Americans had sympathized with the Communist party in the 1930s. At the height of the Great Depression, American Communists were active in progressive causes such as supporting labor unions against the injustices of big corporations, supporting underpaid and mistreated migrant farmworkers, supporting desegregation of black and white communities, and other social issues.

⮕ COMMUNIST SYMPATHIES

The Communists were especially interested in supporting the anti-Fascist forces in the Spanish Civil War. The Spanish Republicans had tried to establish a Communist republic in Spain in 1936, but the Fascists under Francisco Franco had sought to overthrow the republic. The Fascists were supplied with weapons by Nazi Germany while the Spanish Republicans were supported by the Soviet Union. The Spanish Republicans were also supported in their fight against Nazi tyranny by many Americans, some of whom formed the Abraham Lincoln Brigade and went to Spain to fight for the young republic. Oppenheimer had been a big supporter of the Spanish Republicans, sending them money via the American Communist party. In 1942, once he was appointed head of the Los Alamos Laboratory, Oppenheimer cut all of his ties with the American Communist party.

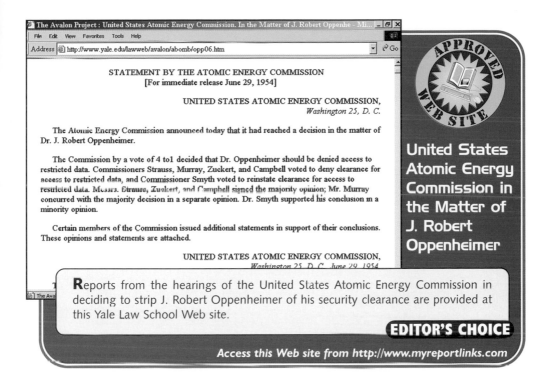

The Avalon Project : United States Atomic Energy Commission. In the Matter of J. Robert Oppenhe - Mi...

File   Edit   View   Favorites   Tools   Help

Address http://www.yale.edu/lawweb/avalon/abomb/opp06.htm ▾ Go

STATEMENT BY THE ATOMIC ENERGY COMMISSION
[For immediate release June 29, 1954]

UNITED STATES ATOMIC ENERGY COMMISSION,
Washington 25, D. C.

The Atomic Energy Commission announced today that it had reached a decision in the matter of Dr. J. Robert Oppenheimer.

The Commission by a vote of 4 to1 decided that Dr. Oppenheimer should be denied access to restricted data. Commissioners Strauss, Murray, Zuckert, and Campbell voted to deny clearance for access to restricted data, and Commissioner Smyth voted to reinstate clearance for access to restricted data. Messrs. Strauss, Zuckert, and Campbell signed the majority opinion; Mr. Murray concurred with the majority decision in a separate opinion. Dr. Smyth supported his conclusion in a minority opinion.

Certain members of the Commission issued additional statements in support of their conclusions. These opinions and statements are attached.

UNITED STATES ATOMIC ENERGY COMMISSION,
Washington 25, D. C. June 29, 1954.

United States
Atomic Energy
Commission in
the Matter of
J. Robert
Oppenheimer

Reports from the hearings of the United States Atomic Energy Commission in deciding to strip J. Robert Oppenheimer of his security clearance are provided at this Yale Law School Web site.

EDITOR'S CHOICE

Access this Web site from http://www.myreportlinks.com

→ THE OPPENHEIMER HEARINGS

In 1953, William Borden, former head of the Joint Congressional Committee on Atomic Energy, wrote a letter to J. Edgar Hoover, the head of the Federal Bureau of Investigation. In the letter, Borden claimed that J. Robert Oppenheimer was "a hardened Communist" and that "more probably than not he has since been functioning as an espionage agent."[5] Hoover notified the White House, and President Dwight Eisenhower cut Oppenheimer off from all work on top secret atomic weapons. The president ordered that a "blank wall be placed between Dr. Oppenheimer and any secret data" concerning atomic weapons, until a hearing could be held determining his guilt or innocence.[6]

That hearing was held in 1954. Oppenheimer claimed that he had not been politically motivated in the early 1930s, before the rise of Nazism. For example, he said, "To many of my friends my indifference to contemporary affairs seemed bizarre. . . . I was deeply interested in my science; but I had no understanding of the relations of man to his society."[7]

When Oppenheimer recalled contributing money to the Communist party, he claimed it had been done for the most innocent reasons: "I doubt that it occurred to me that the [financial] contributions [I made to the Communist party] might be directed to other purposes than those I had intended, or that such purposes might be evil. I

◀ Edward Teller, a physicist and colleague of Oppenheimer's on the Manhattan Project, provided damaging testimony against Oppenheimer during the hearings of 1954. Once friends, the two disagreed on the need for a hydrogen bomb. Teller was in favor of it, while Oppenheimer was opposed to it.

did not then regard Communists as dangerous; and some of their declared objectives seemed to me desirable."[8]

The most damaging testimony against Oppenheimer came from a surprising source. Edward Teller, a top scientist who had worked with Oppenheimer on the Manhattan Project, was outspoken in his attacks on the former head of the Los Alamos Laboratory for his opposition to building the hydrogen bomb. Teller had wanted to work on the development of the hydrogen bomb even while he was working on the atomic bomb, and Oppenheimer had been opposed to a hydrogen bomb's development. Teller's testimony against Oppenheimer angered many in the scientific community, who felt he had betrayed the Manhattan Project's leader.

⮕ THE HEARINGS' AFTERMATH

Oppenheimer was publicly humiliated when at the end of his hearing, the United States government revoked his top secret security clearance. He could no longer work on any programs concerning atomic energy. He was found to be careless when it came to security issues. He was not, however, found guilty of being a spy or a traitor.

This event seriously damaged Oppenheimer's career, cut him off from much of his work, and created a rift between him and scientists such as

Edward Teller, the father of the hydrogen bomb, who were vocal in their anticommunism.

Many in the scientific community and even some in the government and the military came to the defense of J. Robert Oppenheimer. Forty of the top scientists in his field gave evidence at Oppenheimer's hearings of his loyalty to the United States. Of Oppenheimer's patriotism, George Kennan of the Institute for Advanced Study in Princeton, New Jersey, would later say,

> The truth is that the U.S. Government never had a servant more devoted at heart than this one, in the sense of wishing to make a constructive contribution; and I know of nothing more tragic than the series

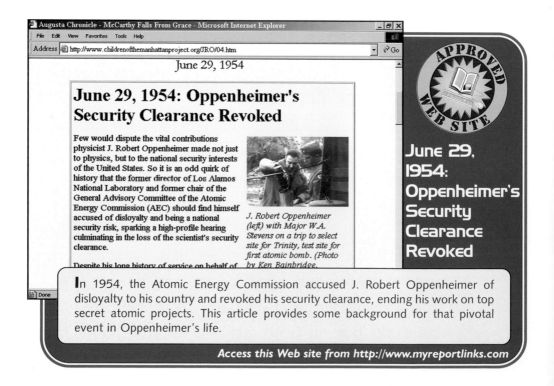

Augusta Chronicle - McCarthy Falls From Grace - Microsoft Internet Explorer

File   Edit   View   Favorites   Tools   Help

Address   http://www.childrenofthemanhattanproject.org/JRO/04.htm   Go

June 29, 1954

June 29, 1954: Oppenheimer's Security Clearance Revoked

Few would dispute the vital contributions physicist J. Robert Oppenheimer made not just to physics, but to the national security interests of the United States. So it is an odd quirk of history that the former director of Los Alamos National Laboratory and former chair of the General Advisory Committee of the Atomic Energy Commission (AEC) should find himself accused of disloyalty and being a national security risk, sparking a high-profile hearing culminating in the loss of the scientist's security clearance.

Despite his long history of service on behalf of

J. Robert Oppenheimer (left) with Major W.A. Stevens on a trip to select site for Trinity, test site for first atomic bomb. (Photo by Ken Bainbridge.

APPROVED WEB SITE

June 29, 1954: Oppenheimer's Security Clearance Revoked

Done

In 1954, the Atomic Energy Commission accused J. Robert Oppenheimer of disloyalty to his country and revoked his security clearance, ending his work on top secret atomic projects. This article provides some background for that pivotal event in Oppenheimer's life.

Access this Web site from http://www.myreportlinks.com

of mistakes . . . that obliged him to spend the last decade and a half of his life eating out his heart in frustration . . . There was, I suspect, no conviction he held more dearly—none that meant more to him—than the belief that the science of nuclear physics harboured possibilities for communication and understanding among men as exciting in their way as its destructive possibilities were terrifying. It was one of the great disappointments of his [Oppenheimer's] life that he was permitted at the official level to contribute so greatly to the one [the making of the atomic bomb], not at all to the other [of finding a way to world peace].[9]

In the end, despite those who spoke eloquently on Oppenheimer's behalf, his critics were able to capitalize on the anti-Communist hysteria of the time and Oppenheimer's own failures in judgment. The man who had built the atomic bomb was banned from working on atomic projects for the United States government for the rest of his life.

LAST YEARS

Oppenheimer's career went into decline after his government security clearance was taken away. He had almost no major influence on the development of the nuclear age after 1954. He never wrote another scientific paper after 1950. He did, however, continue working in science and continued to inspire those who studied under him. From 1947 to 1966, Oppenheimer was the director of the Institute for Advanced Study in Princeton, New Jersey, the longtime workplace of physicist Albert Einstein. While there, Oppenheimer oversaw the research of two hundred postdoctoral fellows in many fields of study. He toured Europe, lectured, and wrote several books, including *Science and the Common Understanding* in 1954 and *Some Reflections on Science and Culture* in 1960. He also spent several months a year

CHAPTER

6

vacationing with his family on the island of St. John in the Virgin Islands.

→ A PRESTIGIOUS AWARD

Oppenheimer was not totally forgotten by his government, the public, or his colleagues. In 1963, for example, he was honored by President Lyndon Johnson with the $50,000 Enrico Fermi Award for "outstanding contributions to theoretical physics and his scientific and administrative leadership."[1] Referring to all the anti-Communists who opposed him and had wrongly considered him a security risk, Oppenheimer told President Johnson, "I think it is just possible, Mr. President, that it has taken some charity and some courage for you to make this award [to me] today."[2] Despite that award,

▲ Although no longer involved in nuclear research, Dr. Oppenheimer continued to inspire and mentor young scientists in his position as the director of the Institute for Advanced Study, where he worked for nearly twenty years.

Oppenheimer's security clearance was never restored.

In 1965, Oppenheimer returned briefly to Los Alamos to give a memorial address for physicist Niels Bohr, who had died in 1962. The former head of the Los Alamos Lab received a thunderous standing ovation from the scientists at work there.

⊜ LAST DAYS

By 1965, Oppenheimer's health began to fail. He retired as director of the Institute for Advanced Study, although he accepted a position as senior professor of theoretical physics. Years of smoking undoubtedly contributed to the throat cancer that finally claimed his life on February 18, 1967, in Princeton.

Just five years later, in 1972, Oppie's prediction of the existence of black holes was verified by astronomers.

→THE ATOMIC BOMB'S LEGACY

Today we continue to live with J. Robert Oppenheimer's legacy: with both his greatest successes as a weapons maker and his greatest failures as a peacemaker. The threat of nuclear war and the end of civilization still hangs over our heads, with not enough having been done to curb the development and production of weapons of mass destruction.

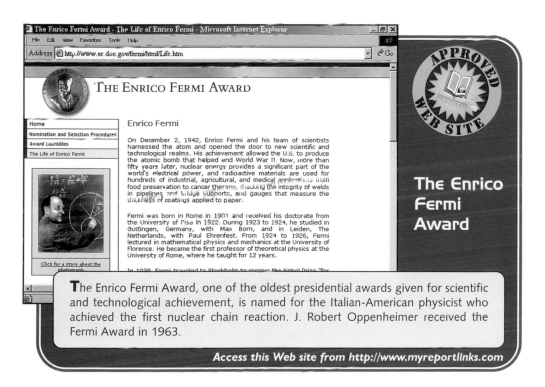

The Enrico Fermi Award, one of the oldest presidential awards given for scientific and technological achievement, is named for the Italian-American physicist who achieved the first nuclear chain reaction. J. Robert Oppenheimer received the Fermi Award in 1963.

Access this Web site from http://www.myreportlinks.com

▲ *Dr. J. Robert Oppenheimer, father of the atomic bomb, spent his last days in the serene atmosphere of academic life.*

As nations such as North Korea and Iran try to join the "nuclear club" of atomic bomb-possessing nations, the risk that atomic bombs will again be used against innocent people increases. The failure of governments to adopt Oppenheimer's plans for the control of nuclear weapons also means that such weapons could more easily fall into the hands of terrorists.

Humanity's greatest hope is that the terrible power unleashed by a team of brilliant scientists working under perhaps the most brilliant of them all, J. Robert Oppenheimer, will never be used in wartime again.

Activities for the Nuclear Age

This chapter offers activities to help you understand some of the science and social issues surrounding the work of J. Robert Oppenheimer, the scientist behind the building of the atomic bomb.

How Small Is an Atom?

It is difficult for us to imagine the microworld of molecules and atoms. In this activity, you can begin to get a hint of just how tiny an atom really is.

You will need an 11-inch-long (28-centimeter-long) strip of paper and a pair of scissors.

Cut the paper in half over and over again, thirty-one times in all, until it is reduced to the size of an atom, or roughly .0000000045 inch. Of course this is not really possible, but imagine that you can do it, and you will begin to get an idea of how small an atom really is. Albert Einstein called such an experiment a "thought experiment," since its result can only be imagined.

Cut #1 puts you at 5.5 inches (14 centimeters), about the length of a pen. Cut #2 takes you to 2.75 inches (7 centimeters), about the length of a finger. Cut #3 puts you at 1.38 inches (3.5 centimeters), about the length of a matchstick. Cut #4 takes you to .69 inch (1.75 centimeters), about the diameter of a dime. Cut #5 takes you to .345 inch (0.877 centimeter), about the diameter of a pea.

Cut #6 reduces the length of the piece of paper to .17 inch (0.44 centimeter), about the length of a large ant. Cut #7 takes the paper down to 0.085 inch (0.22 centimeter), about the thickness of a piece of string. Cut #8 reduces the length of the paper to .04 inch (1 millimeter), the size of a small plant seed. Cut #9 puts the size of the paper at .02 inch (0.5 millimeter), the thickness of a piece of thread. Cut #10 puts the paper's length at .01 inch (0.25 millimeter), which is usually about as far as anyone can cut with scissors.

You can then begin to enter a miniature world that can only be imagined. Cut #12 (if it could be done) would put the paper at .002 inch (.05 millimeter), about the width of a human hair. Cut #18, if you can imagine it, takes it to .0004 inch (10 microns), about the size of a bacterium seen only through a microscope.

At Cut #19, the length of the piece of paper would be .000018 inch (.5 micron), the size of visible light waves like those from the sun. At Cut

#24, you would arrive at .0000006 inch (.015 micron), the range of size that the best electron microscopes can see.

And finally at Cut #31, the piece of paper is reduced to the diameter of an atom, .0000000045 inch (0.0001 micron). Still, as small as this is, one needs to realize that most of the atom is just empty space, and that the subatomic particles—electrons, protons, and neutrons—are many times smaller than the atom itself.

Realizing just how small the atom and its subatomic particles are, you can begin to comprehend just how difficult it was for theoretical physicists to create a working model of the atom and its components. It was the accuracy of those physicists' calculations that made the atomic bomb possible.[1]

Activity #2

Making a Planetary Model of an Atom

Atoms are the basic building blocks of matter. There are now 110 known fundamental atoms, making up 110 elements.

In this activity, you will build a planetary model of a carbon atom, as scientists imagined the atom to look before quantum mechanics changed our precise view of the atom. We picked a carbon atom because it is a simple stable atom, with just six electrons distributed over two orbits, and six protons and six neutrons found in the nucleus. (By comparison, the uranium 235 used in the atomic bomb contains 143 neutrons and 92 protons.)

To make a carbon atom planetary model, you need six large yellow gumdrops to represent neutrons, six large green gumdrops to represent protons, and six small red gumdrops to represent electrons. You also need several toothpicks to hold your atom together.

Start by assembling the carbon atom nucleus. It contains six neutrons (yellow gumdrops) and six protons (green gumdrops). Mold the neutrons and protons (yellow and green gumdrops) together tightly to form the nucleus of the atom.

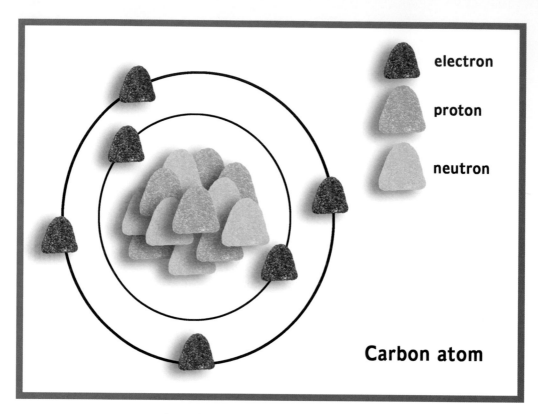

electron

proton

neutron

Carbon atom

Next, break a toothpick in half. Place one of the electrons (small red gumdrops) at one end of the broken toothpick. Then stick the other end of the toothpick into the nucleus. Add a second electron in the same way. This completes the first electron ring around the carbon atom (containing two electrons).

Now take a whole toothpick and place one of the electrons (small red gumdrops) at one end. Stick the other end of the toothpick into the nucleus. Do the same with three more electrons (small red gumdrops), mounting them on full-length toothpicks, then sticking them into the nucleus.

You now have a planetary model of a carbon atom, with its nucleus of six protons and six neutrons, a first orbit of two electrons, and a second orbit of four electrons.

If you can imagine this carbon atom as a more complex U-235 atom, you might be able to understand how J. Robert Oppenheimer and the Los Alamos scientists split the atom and created the atomic bomb. What they did was to hit the nucleus of the U-235 atom with an independent neutron. That neutron broke the nucleus apart, releasing other neutrons and some of the energy that bonded the nucleus together (the stickiness of the gumdrops). Those released neutrons hit other nuclei, breaking them apart, releasing more neutrons and more energy, causing a rapid chain reaction, and a massive release of nuclear energy in the form of a fission atomic bomb explosion.

Activity #3

The Modern City and the Atomic Bomb

This activity looks at the development of the atomic bomb from two points of view: first, from the viewpoint of those who built the bomb, and then from the viewpoint of those who were bombed. It also shows how difficult it would be to live in a city hit with an atomic bomb.

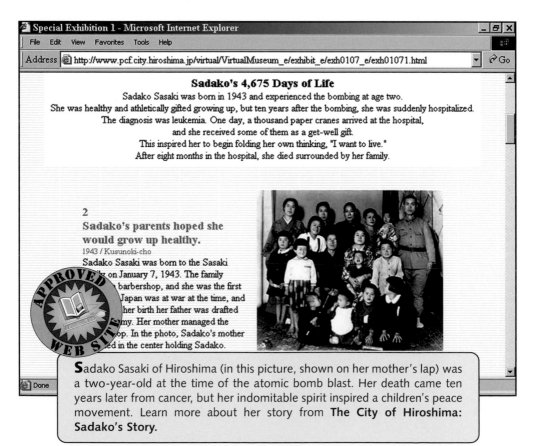

Special Exhibition 1 - Microsoft Internet Explorer

File   Edit   View   Favorites   Tools   Help

Address http://www.pcf.city.hiroshima.jp/virtual/VirtualMuseum_e/exhibit_e/exh0107_e/exh01071.html

Sadako's 4,675 Days of Life

Sadako Sasaki was born in 1943 and experienced the bombing at age two.
She was healthy and athletically gifted growing up, but ten years after the bombing, she was suddenly hospitalized.
The diagnosis was leukemia. One day, a thousand paper cranes arrived at the hospital,
and she received some of them as a get-well gift.
This inspired her to begin folding her own thinking, "I want to live."
After eight months in the hospital, she died surrounded by her family.

2

Sadako's parents hoped she would grow up healthy.

1943 / Kusunoki-cho

Sadako Sasaki was born to the Sasaki ... on January 7, 1943. The family ... barbershop, and she was the first ... Japan was at war at the time, and ... her birth her father was drafted ... my. Her mother managed the ... op. In the photo, Sadako's mother ... d in the center holding Sadako.

Sadako Sasaki of Hiroshima (in this picture, shown on her mother's lap) was a two-year-old at the time of the atomic bomb blast. Her death came ten years later from cancer, but her indomitable spirit inspired a children's peace movement. Learn more about her story from **The City of Hiroshima: Sadako's Story.**

Divide your class in half. One half builds a city out of clay, cardboard boxes, construction paper, and other materials. Make the city as realistic as you can, and label each building: city hall, school, hospital, post office, police station, supermarket, homes, and so on.

The other half of the group prepares an "atomic bomb" (built out of clay or other simple materials). Both sides work hard to build their projects. Then the "bombers" come in and destroy the city by dropping the "bomb."

Afterward, talk about how it felt to be bombed, and how it felt to be the bombers. Also talk about what it would be like to try and live without your city or town hall, school, hospital, post office, police station, supermarkets, schools, and homes. Then repeat the experiment by swapping roles with each other.

Activity #4

"Quantum Leaps" and the Tipping Point for Peace

In 1955, an eleven-year-old girl from Hiroshima, Japan, named Sadako Sasaki discovered that she had leukemia, a disease in which the body produces an abnormal number of white blood cells. That disease was most likely caused by the radiation from the uranium atomic bomb dropped on Hiroshima on August 6, 1945. Sadako was given only a few months to live.

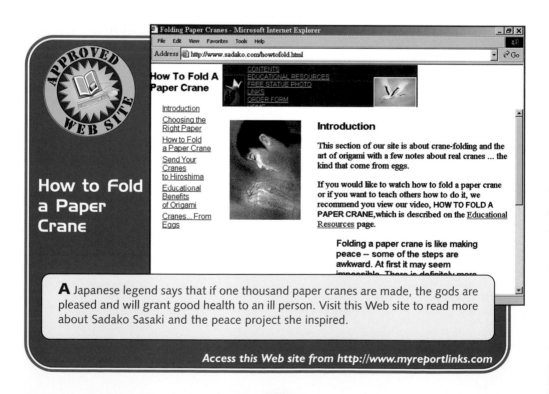

A Japanese legend says that if one thousand paper cranes are made, the gods are pleased and will grant good health to an ill person. Visit this Web site to read more about Sadako Sasaki and the peace project she inspired.

Access this Web site from http://www.myreportlinks.com

Sadako Sasaki's friend told her of an old legend: If a person made one thousand folded paper cranes, whatever that person wished for would come true. Sadako made the cranes in hopes that she would live. Sadly, she died. But in her death, she inspired a worldwide movement for peace focused on the making of paper "peace cranes" by children.

In this exercise see how the idea of peace can catch on with your friends and classmates, and spread by "quantum leaps."

Start by learning how to make a paper peace crane by going to the How to Fold a Paper Crane Web page. It is one of the recommended Report Links for this book, found at **www.myreportlinks.com.** You might also go to the Hiroshima International School Web site to see their paper-folding instructions.[3]

Once you have learned how to make a paper peace crane, teach a friend or classmate how to make his or her own crane. The finished cranes can be displayed at your school, made part of a community peace celebration, or even contributed to Hiroshima's Peace Park.

Report Links

The Internet sites described below can be accessed at
http://www.myreportlinks.com

▶**J. Robert Oppenheimer Centennial at Berkeley**
Editor's ChoiceA university Web site takes a look back at the life of J. Robert Oppenheimer.

▶**Los Alamos National Laboratory: The Road to Los Alamos**
Editor's Choice This Los Alamos National Laboratory site offers a history of the Manhattan Project.

▶*Race for the Superbomb:* **People and Events**
Editor's Choice A PBS site examines the major players in the development of the hydrogen bomb.

▶**United States Atomic Energy Commission in the Matter of J. Robert Oppenheimer**
Editor's Choice Read the text of the AEC's case against Oppenheimer.

▶**Trinity Remembered**
Editor's Choice This site recalls the first test of a nuclear weapon.

▶**Nuclear Files.org**
Editor's Choice Learn about the history of nuclear weapons.

▶**Alsos Digital Library for Nuclear Issues**
This site offers information on more than two thousand resources about nuclear topics.

▶**Argonne National Laboratory**
Learn about the lab where Enrico Fermi and his team produced the first nuclear chain reaction.

▶**The Atomic Age: From Fission to Fallout**
Learn about the early history of the atomic bomb.

▶**Atomic Archive**
Images of the first nuclear weapon test and other photographs are featured on this site.

▶**The Atomic Bombings of Hiroshima and Nagasaki**
Read an official report of the damage wrought by the atomic bombs dropped on Japan in 1945.

▶**Atomic Heritage Foundation:** *Life* **Magazine, October 10, 1949**
Read this *Life* magazine article on J. Robert Oppenheimer.

▶**The City of Hiroshima: Sadako's Story**
Learn how a girl's death from cancer caused by the bombing of Hiroshima inspired a peace movement.

▶**The Cuban Missile Crisis, 1962: The Fortieth Anniversary**
George Washington University focuses on the Cuban Missile Crisis.

▶*Enola Gay*
Learn more about the plane that dropped the atomic bomb on Hiroshima.

Report Links

The Internet sites described below can be accessed at
http://www.myreportlinks.com

▶**The Enrico Fermi Award**
Find out more about an award given to Dr. J. Robert Oppenheimer in 1963.

▶**Final Report of the Advisory Committee on Human Radiation Experiments**
Read a revealing examination of human radiation experiments in America.

▶**The 40's**
Learn about the beginnings of the atomic age.

▶**Frank Oppenheimer: Founder of the Exploratorium**
Read a biography of Frank Oppenheimer, J. Robert Oppenheimer's brother.

▶**How Atoms Work**
A tutorial on atoms, the basic units of our universe, is offered on this site.

▶**How to Fold a Paper Crane**
A young bomb victim's legacy is profiled.

▶**J. Robert Oppenheimer**
A biographical memoir of J. Robert Oppenheimer by a fellow physicist can be found on this site.

▶**June 29, 1954: Oppenheimer's Security Clearance Revoked**
This site offers information about J. Robert Oppenheimer's loss of security clearance.

▶**Los Alamos Historical Society: The Manhattan Project**
This historical society site offers information on Los Alamos in the 1940s.

▶**The Manhattan Project: An Interactive History**
This government site offers a comprehensive history of the Manhattan Project.

▶**Manhattan Project Who's Who**
Five key scientists involved in the Manhattan Project are profiled on this site.

▶*Nazis and the Bomb*
This PBS Web site looks at Hitler's nuclear program.

▶**A Photo-Essay on the Bombing of Hiroshima and Nagasaki**
This article combines text and photos to tell the stories of Hiroshima and Nagasaki.

▶**"Regarding Scientist X"**
The *Berkeley Science Review* has an article on Communist activity at Berkeley's Radiation Lab.

▶**When Bomb Shelters Were All the Rage**
This *Detroit News* article takes a look back at bomb shelters.

atom—The smallest particle of an element.

atomic pile—An early form of nuclear reactor designed to create a sustained fission reaction. In such a reaction, the nucleus or center of an atom is split in two, creating two new nuclei, and so on, releasing large amounts of energy slowly.

black hole—Occurs in outer space when a super-massive star collapses on itself. Its matter becomes so dense, and its gravity so intense, that nothing can ever escape from it, not even light.

chain reaction—A series of events in which each event causes the next. In an atomic reaction, subatomic particles released by one split atomic nucleus trigger the splitting or fission of the next, and so on.

Cold War—The period of history from 1945 to 1991 when the United States and Soviet Union challenged each other for world supremacy.

critical mass—The minimum amount of fissionable material, such as uranium 235 or plutonium, needed to cause an atomic chain reaction.

electron—One of three basic subatomic particles that make up the atom. An electron spins around an atom's nucleus and has a negative charge.

gamma rays—High-energy radiation particles released by an atomic bomb causing radiation sickness.

isotope—An atom having the same number of protons in its nucleus as other varieties of an element, but with a varying number of neutrons.

kiloton—Multiples of 1,000 tons, usually used to describe the number of tons of dynamite equivalent to the force of a nuclear explosion.

molecular spectrum—Shows the energy emitted by a radiant source, like a star or a burning candle. The rainbow is the sun's spectrum.

nuclear fission—The splitting of an atomic nucleus, resulting in the release of large amounts of energy. Slow fission generates atomic energy in a nuclear reactor. Fast fission results in an atomic explosion.

nuclear proliferation—The spread of nuclear weapon production from one nation to another.

neutron—One of three basic subatomic particles that make up the atom. A neutron is located in the nucleus and has no charge. Fast moving neutrons are used to split the atom, resulting in nuclear fission.

neutron star—The collapsed core of a massive star that remains after a supernova explosion. A neutron star is so dense, and so tightly packed, that all of its atoms have collapsed, with only atomic nuclei remaining.

physics—The science of matter and energy and their interactions.

plutonium—A fissionable element, heavier than uranium, first discovered early in 1941.

proton—One of three basic subatomic particles that make up the atom. A proton is located in the nucleus and has a positive charge.

quantum mechanics—The study of how the universe works at very small scales, especially looking at how subatomic particles such as electrons, protons, and neutrons behave within an atom.

radiation sickness—Deadly disease caused by exposure to radioactivity.

radioactive—The emission of alpha, beta, or gamma rays from an atom.

uranium 235 (U-235)—An isotope of the element uranium used in the atomic bomb. It contains 143 neutrons and 92 protons in its nucleus.

uranium gun—The mechanism of the uranium atomic bomb. It employs a modified artillery gun with a small explosive charge that can propel a subcritical piece of uranium down a "gun barrel" into a second subcritical piece of uranium. When the two pieces come together, they have the required critical mass to cause an atomic bomb detonation.

Chapter 1. Fire in the Desert

1. William Manchester, *The Glory and the Dream* (New York: Bantam Books, 1975), pp. 377–378.

2. J. Robert Oppenheimer Centennial, Office for History of Science and Technology, The University of California at Berkeley, *Oppenheimer: A Life,* p. 18, 2004, <http://ohst.berkeley.edu/oppenheimer/exhibit/printedition-lowres.pdf> (July 14, 2006).

3. Manchester, p. 378.

Chapter 2. Early Years

1. Kai Bird and Martin J. Sherwin, *American Prometheus: The Triumph and Tragedy of J. Robert Oppenheimer* (New York: Alfred A. Knopf, 2005), p. 15.

2. J. Robert Oppenheimer Centennial, Office for History of Science and Technology, The University of California at Berkeley, *Oppenheimer: A Life,* "The Early Years," 2004, <http://ohst.berkeley.edu/oppenheimer/exhibit/chapter1.html> (April 20, 2006).

3. Peter Goodchild, *J. Robert Oppenheimer, Shatterer of Worlds* (New York: Fromm International Publishing Corporation, 1985), p. 12.

4. Bird and Sherwin, p. 15.

5. Goodchild, p. 12.

6. Ibid., p. 15.

7. Ibid., p. 16.

8. Bird and Sherwin, p. 64.

9. Ibid., p. 65.

10. Ibid., p. 73.

11. Ibid.

12. Bird and Sherwin, p. 89.

13. *New York Times,* Obituary, "J. Robert Oppenheimer, Atom Bomb Pioneer, Dies," February 19, 1967.

Chapter 3. Oppenheimer and the Manhattan Project

1. *A History of Quantum Mechanics,* n.d., <http://www-groups.dcs.st-and.ac.uk/~history/HistTopics/The_Quantum_age_begins.html> (April 20, 2006).

2. Richard Rhodes, *The Making of the Atomic Bomb* (New York: Simon and Schuster, 1986), p. 314.

3. Peter Goodchild, *J. Robert Oppenheimer, Shatterer of Worlds* (New York: Fromm International Publishing Corporation, 1985), p. 45.

4. Los Alamos National Laboratory, "50th Anniversary Article: New Weapons Laboratory Gives Birth to the 'Gadget,' " n.d., <http://www.lanl.gov/history/atomicbomb/gadget-born.shtml> (April 20, 2006).

5. Kai Bird and Martin J. Sherwin, *American Prometheus: The Triumph and Tragedy of J. Robert Oppenheimer* (New York: Alfred A. Knopf, 2005), p. 291.

6. Stephane Groueff, *Manhattan Project: The Untold Story of the Making of the Atomic Bomb* (Boston: Little, Brown and Company, 1967), p. 355.

Chapter 4. Life After the Atomic Bomb

1. William Manchester, *The Glory and the Dream* (New York: Bantam Books, 1975), p. 379.

2. Richard Rhodes, *The Making of the Atomic Bomb* (New York: Simon and Schuster, 1986), p. 704.

3. Ibid., p. 710.

4. Ibid., p. 711.

5. Ibid.

6. Ibid., pp. 714–715.

7. Ibid., p. 719.

8. Ibid.

9. Atomicarchive.com, "Eyewitness Account of Atomic Bomb Over Nagasaki," n.d., <http://www.atomicarchive.com/Docs/Hiroshima/Nagasaki.shtml> (April 20, 2006).

10. Los Alamos Study Group, "Historical Objections from Scientists Working on the First Bomb," n.d., <http://www.lasg.org/LifeAtTheLabs/objections.htm> (April 20, 2006).

11. Atomicarchive.com, "Cuban Missile Crisis," n.d., <http://www.atomicarchive.com/Docs/Cuba/index.shtml> (April 20, 2006).

Chapter 5. From Hero to Villain

1. *New York Times,* Obituary, "J. Robert Oppenheimer, Atom Bomb Pioneer, Dies," February 19, 1967.

2. Ibid.

3. Ibid.

4. J. Robert Oppenheimer Centennial, Office for History of Science and Technology, The University of California at Berkeley, *Oppenheimer: A Life,* "A Changed World," 2004, <http://ohst.berkeley.edu/oppenheimer/exhibit/text/ch4page1.html> (April 20, 2006).

5. *New York Times,* Obituary, "J. Robert Oppenheimer, Atom Bomb Pioneer, Dies," February 19, 1967.

6. Ibid.

7. Kai Bird and Martin J. Sherwin, *American Prometheus: The Triumph and Tragedy of J. Robert Oppenheimer* (New York: Alfred A. Knopf, 2005), p. 104.

8. Ibid., p. 123.

9. Abraham Pais, *J. Robert Oppenheimer, A Life* (New York: Oxford University Press, 2006), p. 306.

Chapter 6. Last Years

1. *New York Times,* Obituary, "J. Robert Oppenheimer, Atom Bomb Pioneer, Dies," February 19, 1967.

2. J. Robert Oppenheimer Centennial, Office for History of Science and Technology, The University of California at Berkeley, *Oppenheimer: A Life,* "The Price of Security," 2004, <http://ohst.berkeley.edu/oppenheimer/exhibit/chapter5.html> (April 20, 2006).

Activities for the Nuclear Age

1. The Atoms Family, "The Phantom's Portrait Parlor, Paper Cutting," n.d., <http://www.miamisci.org/af/sln/phantom/papercutting.html> (April 20, 2006).

2. Hiroshima International School, "How to Fold a Crane," n.d., <http://www.hiroshima-is.ac.jp/Hiroshima/foldcrai.htm> (April 20, 2006).

Allman, Toney. *J. Robert Oppenheimer: Theoretical Physicist, Atomic Pioneer.* Detroit: Blackbirch Press, 2005.

Crewe, Sabrina, and Dale Anderson. *The Atom Bomb Project.* Milwaukee: Gareth Stevens Publishers, 2005.

Cullen, Katherine. *Science, Technology, and Society: The People Behind the Science.* New York: Facts on File, 2006.

Fleisher, Paul. *Relativity and Quantum Mechanics: Principles of Modern Physics.* Minneapolis: Lerner Publications Co., 2002.

Greenspan, Nancy Thorndike. *The End of the Certain World: The Life and Science of Max Born.* New York: Basic Books, 2005.

Ishi, Takayuki. *One Thousand Paper Cranes: The Story of Sadako and the Children's Peace Statue.* New York: Random House, 1997.

Lawton, Clive A. *Hiroshima: The Story of the First Atom Bomb.* Cambridge, Mass.: Candlewick Press, 2004.

Pasachoff, Naomi. *Niels Bohr: Physicist and Humanitarian.* Berkeley Heights, N.J.: Enslow Publishers, Inc., 2003.

Roleff, Tamara L., ed. *The Atom Bomb.* San Diego: Greenhaven Press, 2000.

Sherrow, Victoria. *The Making of the Atom Bomb.* San Diego: Lucent Books, 2000.